THE NEW
ENTREPRENEURS

THE NEW ENTREPRENEURS

Women Working from Home

Terri P. Tepper
and Nona Dawe Tepper

UNIVERSE BOOKS

New York

Published in the United States of America in 1980
by Universe Books
381 Park Avenue South, New York, N.Y. 10016

80 81 82 83 84/10 9 8 7 6 5 4 3 2 1

Printed in the United States of America

Library of Congress Cataloging in Publication Data

Tepper, Terri P
  The new entrepreneurs.

  Interviews with 40 women.
  Includes index.
  1. Women in business—United States—Interviews.
2. Self-employed—United States—Interviews. 3. Home
labor—United States. I. Tepper, Nona Dawe, joint
author. II. Title.
HF5500.3.U54T46   658'.041   80-17578
ISBN 0-87663-342-4

Dedication

To Samuel J. Tepper, husband and father,
who believed in this book and marveled at the
ingenuity of women home entrepreneurs

Contents

Introduction

This book is a composite of 40 personal narratives and documentary portraits of women throughout the United States who operate businesses from their homes. It is a result of my own difficulties in working from home while caring for two children. I wondered if it was possible to operate a home business successfully and felt the best way to find out would be to ask other women how they were coping. Because there is often a condescending attitude toward home business, it was my belief that photographs, particularly documentary portraits, along with narratives, would help show the beauty, the strength, and the dignity of women who, while raising children, sought to generate income and achieve self-fulfillment through a home business.

Over a period of three years, Nona, my mother, and I interviewed and photographed 98 women of all ages and backgrounds, 40 of whom are included in this book. Each interview and photographic session took between two and a half and twelve hours, and during that time together, we relived the start-up and development of the businesses. Some of the women's lives were filled with sadness and struggles so profound that they cried as they remembered their experiences. The severity of their struggles was not limited to the development of their businesses but also included the simultaneous responsibility of trying to keep their families together. Because the business and home roles were so often integrated, we included aspects of both in the text of the narratives.

Humor and fun were also a part of the women's lives. They laughed as they remembered how sure they had been of themselves until they discovered that those early efforts did not always result in sales. And sometimes they laughed as they recalled how they started in business. "My feet hurt," Faa (pronounced "Fay") Casper told us. "I got so tired of leaving my home in shoes and coming back carrying them that I decided to do something about it." We asked Faa what background experience prepared her for shoemaking, and we learned that she has sewn all her life. With a mischievous twinkle, Faa told us, "I even sewed for the community prostitutes. They bought the most glamorous fabrics you can imagine. And I learned a completely new way of clothing construction, easy on, easy off."

As the research progressed, the significance of working from home became clear. Women started home businesses because they wanted to stay at home with their children, or because they were divorced, spouses got sick or died, or jobs were unavailable elsewhere—or because a woman determined she was capable of doing better on her own.

Fifteen of the 98 women had to work from home. They were disabled or too sick, too old or too poor to afford to work at the kinds of jobs they could have gotten. If they had small children, they couldn't afford day care as well as rent and food. They did whatever they could to support themselves and often a family as well. They baby sat, they did laundry or secretarial work until bit by bit their reputations spread and the work came steadily in. Reinforced by modest success, they expanded until they could see with satisfaction that they were operating a profitable, fulfilling business. They were proud..Now they look back at the beginning with a sense of humor and wonder at how they coped. For instance, now netting over $30,000 a year, June Harrison, with nine children, had to provide the sole support for her family because her husband became too ill to work. June answered phones in her answering service while at the same time holding babies in her arms, babysitting for others, and planning how she would get the ironing done for clients who had dropped off their laundry.

Beyond home business, this book is about what happens to some women in only two or three years. The women kept in touch with us through letters, phone calls, and Christmas cards after the initial interview. Whole lives changed around. Some of the women closed down their businesses within two years, while others established new markets and then suddenly found themselves in a position to develop licensing programs as offshoots of the original small home business (as in the case of Coralee Kern's maid service).

Where the struggle was too tough, and the women decided it wasn't worth it and closed down their businesses, they weren't beaten. Not at all. They looked at the experience as personal growth and they were glad for it. Sometimes it cost them relatively little money, while others spent over $40,000 for the experience. They looked at their former businesses exactly as Gail Sheehy suggested in her book, *Passages:* "It will be progress when we come to think of serial careers, not as signifying failure, but as a realistic way to prolong vitality." As Pamela Wilson-Pace said about her bookstore and gallery,

> I haven't had a moment's regret about closing The Open Book, but I am equally glad I had the store for four years. The experience of doing it all myself did wonders for my self-confidence and self-respect. I now feel like I can do anything, and at the age of 28, I feel like I'm just on the brink of my life, with so many options and desires for the years ahead of me.

Because of the energy crisis and the cost of commuting, home businesses appear to be increasing. Computers with the capacity to relay information to a central terminal are being installed in people's homes, thereby increasing productivity by eliminating commuting time, as well as increasing job satisfaction for those who prefer their home environment to that of an outside office.

Although home occupation zoning ordinances are being revised across the country, they continue to be unnecessarily restrictive, and they can become obstacles to almost every home business owner. Los Angeles and Chicago, for instance, virtually prohibit any type business in a residence. Almost every ordinance prohibits the employment of people outside the family and specifies the percentage of floor space that may be allocated to a business. These are nonsense provisions. The only relevant limitation on operating a business from home should be to prohibit the business from changing the character of the neighborhood.*

Home businesses are almost always quiet and unobtrusive—and for good reason. Home business owners don't want to live amid pollution. Like their neighbors, they want to keep the residential environment as peaceful as possible. That's why they live where they do instead of in a commercially zoned area. Supportive home occupation zoning ordinances are one positive way communities across the country can ease the energy crisis and inflation tragedy for some of their constituency. A simple direct supportive ordinance which would still maintain the desired residential nature of a neighborhood would be:

> People may use their residence for an office or workshop as

---

*Exceptions are often made for professionals who may hire an unrelated employee. In addition, people in a nonbusiness situation may hire employees outside the family as maids or gardeners, for example, on a daily basis and not be in violation of an ordinance. These practices could arguably be a violation of equal protection under the law.

long as such a business maintains the residential character of the area.

Actually, we found that neighbors not only were supportive of local home businesses, if they knew about them, but also happy that such services or products could be purchased so close by. Therefore, we feel that if this book does nothing more than stimulate people into amending home occupation zoning regulations to be more responsive to a growing number of people's needs, or encourage zoning boards to grant variances when such variances hurt no one, it will have made a significant contribution on behalf of home business.

The Interstate Commerce Commission's Order MC-37 has already addressed another problem of a legal nature affecting home business. The Order forbids truckers to assess charges on shipments to private residences that differ from rates charged on shipments to commercially zoned locations. As is always true, the implementation process lags behind the law, and some of the women said they were charged extra for residential deliveries after the Order went into effect.

Other problems the women discussed related to the integration of their business into home life and are specifically mentioned in the introductions to the individual narratives. By far the majority of women enjoyed working from their home environment irrespective of the problems.

Since we assumed that women worked from home mainly for the same reason I did—because of children still living at home—it came as a surprise to find that 37 of the women had no children living at home. These women worked from their homes because they didn't need or couldn't afford an outside office, they felt safer, or they simply preferred to work from home. Other reasons are mentioned in the introductions to the individual narratives.

The women freely discussed their husbands' responses to their businesses. Arlene Winkler said, "He encouraged me to go forward with my craft, to move into business, and to be professional." Juanita Bass, who sells antiques, told us, "My husband used to call it junk, and now when he sees me making a few dollars, it's not junk any more." Chris Birchfield said, "When my husband comes in in the morning, he's full of jokes and laughs. It diverts and yet I really don't feel I can say to him, 'I don't want you in the work rooms.' Good God! It's his house, too. But when we're here to work, *we are here to work!*" In several instances, when the women had built up a strong profitable business, they invited their husbands to join them. Donna Spencer, who operates an interior design business in Fruitland, Idaho, told us:

> After years of essentially working alone and needing more help, I asked Dale to quit his job and work with me. That was probably the hardest decision that he has ever had to make. After he agreed, we found it wasn't easy to get used to each other on a 24-hour-a-day basis. After a while, though, we wished we had done it years earlier because it's really been a lot better for all of us. Because of Dale, we've expanded.

Raising capital for the businesses was an area of particular concern to us. As director of the Consumer Credit Project, a nonprofit counseling organization concerned with women's credit rights, which I direct from my home, I knew that the credit industry had not opened its doors to women on an equal basis with men. Since home businesses generally start small and a large start-up capital is often unnecessary, we found that many of the women borrowed small amounts from their parents and sometimes from friends. Divorce settlements were another primary source of start-up capital, as were savings accounts the women had built up. Some women used household monies—and usually they felt pretty guilty about it. Very few actually went to banks, and of those, some were successful while others suffered humiliation or from a patronizing attitude. Many of the businesses financed themselves through profits.

Significantly, although the owners of some of the businesses grossed up to a half a million dollars and several netted more than $30,000, making a lot of money was not the most important goal for many of them. Still, it was important to make enough money to be able to afford the business. As Kristin Anderson, a self-supporting artist and metalsmith, said:

> I don't make enough money. Who does? But I really don't! And if I wanted to make money, I wouldn't be doing this. I'd be doing something else. But it is important for me to make enough money doing this that I can do it.

Older women continued to work from home because it kept them active, motivated, and vital. Sixty-nine-year-old Peggy Whitmill, who supports herself by operating a craft shop from her garage in Idaho Falls, Idaho, told us:

> I've thought about retiring. Then I go visit my friends and relatives and they seem to be ailing, and all they do is sit

around and think about themselves and their pains and their aches, and I tell myself, "Well, now, if I didn't have to get up this morning, I'd probably lie in bed, and it wouldn't be long till I'd be like them, so I've just got to keep going, because I've got too many things I want to see. I'm afraid that if I give up, then I'll get lazy and get like them, so each year I say, "Next year I'm going to retire."

Three of the women we interviewed were absolutely destitute. Phyllis Huffman, who became divorced after twenty years of marriage and had to support her three children, told us:

I could not find a job. No steady job at all! I learned how to beg and "crawl" for work. I was either overqualified or underqualified, and no one would hire me. I've never gone through anything like that before and it was horrible. It was one of the worst nightmares I've ever been through. My home business encompassed anything and everything I could do, and it became a fourteen-hour-a-day job, seven days a week. I turned the business into survival. I worked at anything I could get. That included stuffing envelopes for a bank and investigating health spas for an auditor. I did anything I could find along with the hypnosis, the astrology, the numerology, and the editing. I didn't make much money, but I made enough to survive and we never went on welfare.

Tragedy in fact was a part of many of the women's lives. Businesses were launched because of a tragedy—a disability, the death of a spouse, a woman suddenly finding herself alone to raise the family. Home businesses helped dissipate the traumas, and as the women developed their businesses their lives took on renewed meaning.

This book is about women's dreams and aspirations, the implementation of plans, the successes and the failures. The women talk about their frustrations, reassess their business objectives, and show how their businesses mesh with their goals in life. What they have to say will be of interest and benefit to anyone interested in creative thinking and problem solving.

T.P.T. □

Jean Ray Laury

DESIGNER, CRAFTSWOMAN, LECTURER,
TEACHER, WRITER, MAIL ORDER BUSINESS OWNER,
Fresno, California.

Often women with talent and motivation can't seem to get a business started. We found that the women we interviewed had tailored their businesses around a particular interest or talent. They were willing to take risks and establish goals. The longevity of their businesses depended upon their ability to alter nonprofitable business practices and their willingness to persevere.

Jean Ray Laury recognized barriers craftswomen often impose upon themselves in their own homes, and through her writing and lectures she has assisted artists and craftswomen in overcoming barriers so that they can get on with their work.

The Creative Woman's Getting-It-All-Together At Home Handbook is the first book I've written that is in no way a craft book. I wrote it because when I was lecturing and teaching, the questions I was being asked had to do with how I found the time for doing all that I do. I could see that a lot of women were really puzzling and struggling with the question of the importance of their work and that this ultimately involved finding time for themselves. The more I thought about it, the more intrigued I became with this whole issue:

The questions reflected a quandary about setting priorities, as well as tremendous concern over messes in the house and husbands' reactions to messes. The questions seemed to indicate that women felt themselves to be at the mercy of other people's whims and needs. I'm convinced that combining a commitment to a career or some kind of professional dedication with a commitment to home and family can exist happily together. I could never have gotten through life without my work, but I couldn't have lived without my family, either. I wouldn't have wanted to give up either one, and I'm convinced that women should not have to make that choice. Both are possible—they have to be, for women to remain productive and sane and to live fully.

I went to school in Iowa and got my B.A. in art at what was essentially a teacher's college. I studied art and English there and later taught junior high and high school art and literature. I worked at UCLA for a couple of years in the meteorology department plotting weather maps. I wanted to live around the UCLA campus, and that happened to be the job that was available. I married and went to Stanford to do graduate work and got an M.A. in design. I did my first fiber work at Stanford. A child's quilt opened up a whole new world to me.

I did an appliqué quilt at a time when it was unheard of to work with appliqué. Doing the quilt led me into some new work, and I had my first one-woman show. I also had some things in traveling shows and so got into exhibition almost immediately. When I look at the work now, it seems very naive and kind of oversimplified. Still, it all has to start somewhere.

At the same time, I had always wanted to write but never had the courage. All the time I was in college I assumed that everybody who was taking writing classes was a gifted writer and that I would be a plodder, so I never had the nerve to take a writing class. One of the jurors in a quilt competition I entered back East was Roxa Wright, a crafts editor at *House Beautiful*, and she commissioned me to write an article for the magazine. I enjoyed writing the article so much and it was so well received that I was encouraged to go ahead with my writing.

I did a series of nine or ten craft books. Some of them I feel much more strongly about because they are more personal. When I was asked by a publisher to write on a certain subject, I found I didn't have the same personal involvement that I did with books I initiated. For instance, one of the nicest books I've worked on is called *Handmade Toys and Games*. Philosophically I particularly like it because of what it says about play and the function of play in human life. The book sold very, very poorly so I feel there's little connection between the quality of the book itself and what eventually became of it.

I now have four major jobs: (1) designing and producing commissioned works, (2) lecturing and teaching workshops, (3) writing, and (4) selling art and craft books through mail order. The commission work usually involves murals, but sometimes I do small-scale pieces designed for either private or commercial buildings. I also design for magazines. I lecture and teach through a variety of groups and institutions: women's groups such as The Dental Wives Association, or chapters of organized craft groups such as The Embroiderers Guild of America (EGA), The National Standard Council (NSC — another embroiderers' group). The American Crafts Council, and several others: or through community colleges and universities.

I went into the mail order business for my craft books because the books were hard to find and I would get letters over and over from people saying, "I can't find such and such a book," or "I've looked everywhere," or "The bookstores tell me this is out of print." Sometimes it was just out of stock. It takes time to answer those letters, even to send a post card. Then I decided to print a listing of my books and distribute them on a small basis myself. One of the books went out of print, and the publisher decided not to reprint the book. I bought out all of the remaining stock. I have now done that on three books. I'd like the books to bring in more income which will free me in other areas.

Although I taught for one semester at Fresno State University and I have taken other college teaching jobs for short times, I like being at home. My wanting very much to be at home with my children while they were small may have something to do with why I took the direction I did. I don't think it's an accident that I quilt.

There are some kinds of work that give your children access to you when they're small. Most things that I like to do best can be done in an isolated way, like designing or writing or quilting. It's physically possible to combine them with child rearing.

I found I could never write or type while the children were around when they were little. I could sew, because that gave them verbal access. Being at the typewriter, however, is like being on the telephone.

You're so connected into a piece of machinery that it excludes anybody else. Children sense that exclusion very fast, so I would save the writing and typing for a time when they were away or in bed.

I also have a need to spend time with other people, and that's part of why I enjoy the lecturing and teaching. As my children got older, I took on more and more lecturing and workshops. It's been a very gradual transition. When the children were little, I wasn't asked very much, but by the time they were in junior high, I could be gone for a week at a time and it was okay, so it's just been a very convenient arrangement.

Now the primary reason I like working at home is because I really like being my own boss. I have my own schedule. I like to work late at night, and I like to sleep in the morning. I enjoy the home environment.

One of the disadvantages is that you don't really *want* to leave your work, since your work and your pleasure are really the same thing. At the same time, I think there are times when it's important just energy-wise to leave the work. If you're working at home and you have a deadline, you simply tend to work on it 18 hours a day until you finish the job. Anybody who works for herself works longer hours and harder than somebody who doesn't work for herself, but I think she also has more energy for it because her motivations are so different. If you're doing what you want to do with life then of course you've got time for it. That's what your life is for.

It's very difficult to get started because it's so risky and you make yourself so vulnerable. I think it takes a while to develop enough self-confidence to be able to absorb rejection or to reject it so that it doesn't have a negative effect on you. The most important thing for anybody is exposure — any kind of exposure. There's no way you can accomplish anything if there's no exposure for your work.

While you wait for the Metropolitan to invite you to show, you go ahead and show at the local savings and loan, the banks, or the libraries or whatever space is available. All of those are so valuable. A show at a library or a bank may be more valuable than a gallery show because so many people in our society are insecure about art, and if they go to the library and see your work, they feel comfortable. They may discover you!

Women who want to design on commissions need to have their work seen in shows. If they've put up a collection that they think is applicable for interiors, then they need to notify interior designers or decorators or architects. Submitting work by mail is a great way, particularly for beginners, because you don't have to face anybody. It can be a big experience to walk in and propose an exhibit, a commission even, because you stand the chance of being rejected. If you submit by mail, you have the envelope all addressed to send out to the next person before the first one comes back, so you don't even have time to realize the first one has been rejected before the second one's on its way.

Free-lancing is great for women with children. Free-lancing in writing is much the same as free-lancing in designing. Sometimes it involves both. That depends on the philosophic direction of the magazine. If they're showing "how to's" they're not interested in a written article, but if they're interested in a philosophic attitude or approach that accompanies a design, then the writing is very important. Some magazines are more of the decorator type. While they use lots of individually made things, they won't necessarily give the directions for making them. Magazines are tremendous consumers of designs and articles about them. Every month a whole series of magazines come out, and every one of them has a handcrafted fiber work in it. It's a great market.

The most important thing is not to waste your efforts by sending work or photographs of your work to the wrong magazine. That can be avoided by going to the library and simply looking at all the magazines and determining which one your work is most appropriate for, and then writing and making a contact first. It's necessary to identify every scrap of material you send and if possible, to send things that can be left on file. Magazines don't necessarily pick out good ideas as they see them because they so often have a theme for an issue, and if your work doesn't happen to fit that theme and you've requested that your slides or photos be sent back, then that's the end of it. If you leave them on file, six months later they may say, "Oh, we're doing something with all white-on-white this month," and they may remember a certain piece and look it up.

One important thing about selling work is that it offers real feedback. That's society's way of valuing things. Whether or not a woman produces her work with any monetary return in mind, there's no question but that's the way society tells you whether or not your work is worthwhile. I think, therefore, that selling is very important for a woman's own viewpoint of her work. Also, money's important for feeling that you have the freedom to buy the materials you need to work with. Many women seem to have difficulty in convincing themselves that they're worthy of the cost of the materials. When there's a very limited budget, it's hard to spend. If you haven't paid the dentist, it's hard to spend money buying your fabrics, because that seems to be frivolous by comparison, yet it may be every bit as crucial as the bills.

The money that comes from the sale of work absolutely must be kept in a separate fund and go back into the work. That may have to go on for years. If a woman did not have home and family responsibilities, that time span would be condensed and maybe it would just be a matter of a few months, but when her time is so limited, it may be stretched out over a couple of years.

I don't know what has to happen to make people suddenly value themselves, but it seems to be a kind of sudden thing. I would hope it wouldn't take most women as long as it's taken me. I think I've always valued myself and my work, but I don't think I've had adequate confidence in it and, my heavens, I'm 50 years old now. I feel like I'm just arriving at that point where I really feel confident about what I'm doing. I now find it easy to walk into an architect's office or into a gallery and say, "This is what I have," and feel confident about what I have. I now know that if they reject it flatly, it's not going to do me in. I would hope that exposure and experience would provide this for most women.

If I had to offer any advice it would be to risk everything all the time and quit trying to be safe. Once you're willing to risk your whole reputation on something, then you can make a leap forward. That's when you really have the possibility of moving out from whatever you've done before. We spend an awful lot of time defending ourselves and protecting ourselves and being safe and comfortable. If we're expecting to move ahead, we have to take chances and we have to take risks and we have to do things that might make us look foolish if they don't work out, and that's okay. It's all okay. It's okay to be wrong. It's okay to fail if you try something and though, in a certain sense it failed, you're still a winner. You still come out ahead. I don't see how there's any way if you risk things, you can really lose. There's so much that you learn; there's so much of value in what you create.

The Creative Woman's Getting-It-All-Together At Home Handbook is available from Jean Ray Laury, P.O. Box 22, Prather, California 93651. Clothbound, $11.95; paperback, $6.95; plus $1 shipping. California residents add 6% state sales tax.

Pamela Wilson - Pace

RETAIL BOOKSTORE AND
GALLERY OWNER,
Salt Lake City, Utah.

Several of the women we interviewed started their businesses without seeking advice or wanting to research the business.

I had no business experience before I opened my bookstore, and I really had not researched it, which for me, I feel, was the best way to do it. I think if I had checked into it too much, I would not have done it.

Whether or not the business was a financial success, they felt it to be personally rewarding and a significant contribution to their personal growth, which they valued.

I wanted to start some kind of women's center, but I also needed to support myself. I was traveling in California and went into a women's book store, and a woman spent the whole day telling me I should start one. (Hers lasted six months.) She was also working full-time as a nurse and trying to operate her book store as kind of a hobby, and it can't be done. It's more than a full-time job. On vacation in Boston I found a feminist book store, and I copied down the titles of all their books. I knew so little about it that I didn't copy down the names of the publishers. I had to come back here and look up every single book in *Books In Print* and then sort them out according to publishers and order them all. It took me about four months to get it all together. While I waited to receive the books, I worked on the physical space. I painted, carpeted, and built all the shelves myself.

In order to establish a credit rating with publishing companies, I had to prepay all my first orders. I had some money from dividends from my father's company and was able to buy the house and set up the business with that money. My father was then dying, but on some days he was lucid enough that he realized what I was doing. He was very proud of me and very supportive, and that was really important to me.

In October each year, the University of Utah has a women's conference. In 1974 it was held a month before I opened. I had received some shipments by then, so I took what I had to the conference and I sold about $74 worth of books in two days. I thought that was great. At the conference I started my mailing list. I sent invitations to those people when I had my grand opening. That day it was pouring rain. I was out hanging the sign an hour before the opening and thinking no one was going to come, but it was very crowded and I sold a lot. When I went back to the women's conference a year later, I sold $2,500 worth of books.

I attend conferences on the average of one a month, and people save up their shopping knowing that I'll be there. I have a really large birth and child care section, probably almost every book that there is on the subject. I sold those at an OB/GYN nurses' conference, and a nurse asked me if I'd be willing to put out a book list to hand out to her prenatal classes. That's a huge market that isn't seasonal and will always be there, so I'm getting together a book list for such classes at all the hospitals in the state. Recently I sold at a Federally Employed Women's conference. I have women's records also, and I sell them at women's concerts.

Another thing that I've done is expand the bookstore into a gallery. I have a different show by a different woman each month. I take a 25% commission, which is lower than any of the other galleries in town. Nothing is here for more than a month unless I want it to be. It's new exposure for the artists, and new people come into the store to see the artists' work. What's more, as a gallery I get free advertising in the newspapers.

Another form of advertising I feel is valuable is a quarterly newsletter I send out in which I discuss new books. It reminds people that we're here. I get a lot of really good feedback from it. It costs me about $90 to send it out to about 1,500 people. The printing is done on the outside, but I do the collating, addressing, stamping, and sorting myself. A lot of those jobs I do upstairs at home in the evening. I probably should break it all down and see how many hours I really do work.

There aren't any other feminist book stores in Utah, and there aren't any at all in Idaho, Wyoming, or Nevada. There are one or two in Colorado and in Arizona, but I get business from those states, too. There are a lot of books here that are in other stores, but we are the only store that carries only books primarily by or for women. Before I opened, several people asked me, "How can you fill a store with books by women?" Seeing a whole wall of books written by women is a real eye opener for a lot of people.

Some people have told me that they would like to open a feminist book store. A book business takes a lot of capital, and it's extremely low profit. There's an incredible amount of paperwork, and you have to stay on top of it all the time, which includes making returns within the allotted time. There's an abundance of book stores in Salt Lake City, but they're not like this one. Still, the market is very full.

I think I've made the general bookstores get up on their toes especially in their children's sections. My children's section now accounts for almost half the business I do. That section has books written by both men and women.

I started out having totally nonsexist books, but I found that children don't really like the ones written to be nonsexist. They're usually not attractive enough because they're low cost, staple-bound books. Now more and more of the big publishing companies are aware of publishing nonsexist things, but still the children aren't really thrilled with them. There's a lot of good science books or craft books that are neutral, so I started stocking more of those, and we have over 50 different coloring books.

I stock some great literature that is sexist, but I think it should be read because it is fine literature. A lot of the fairy tales put women in an inferior role, but I don't think they can be totally eliminated from children's reading. I will not sell Richard Scarry books because, although they're very popular and good learning books, they are extremely sexist. Some of Dr. Seuss are good and some are bad. I don't generally carry them because I try to stick to books that other stores don't regularly carry.

There's an elementary school a block away from here, and a lot of kids come by after school. They don't buy a lot, but I don't care. I encourage browsing and reading. No one really takes advantage. The children know they can't eat or drink while they are reading the books. Only two books have been so shopworn that I didn't think they could be sold, but a school finally bought them. One was *Great Comic Book Heroes* and the other was *Where Did I Come From*, which is a facts-of-life book. Otherwise, the children's books don't get any more shopworn than the rest do.

What I really want to do now is stay this size and start making money. I grew very quickly. I put about $30,000 into this business, and in the first year I was constantly having to bail myself out. When the bills got to be too much, I put in more money. I've used it up now. There's no more space to grow down here. My husband and I have started working on the rest of the house, and we want to live in it.

Also, I don't know whether it's just that I've been open two years or if it's getting married and sharing my time, or whether it was incorporating, but somehow, over this past year, I have felt the need to separate myself from this business more. I guess I've been in business long enough now that the romance of it has worn off and the hard cold facts have to be faced.

A friend and I have started the Women's Entrepreneurs' Association. She owns a plant store, and she and I were at the same place where we needed a support group of other women who could talk about general business problems and the specific problems of being a woman in business.

Two years later The Open Book went out of business after operating at a financial loss for four years. Some time after that, Pamela wrote:

I have mixed feelings now. I haven't had a moment's regret about closing The Open Book, but I am equally glad I had the store for four years. The experience of doing it all myself did wonders for my self-confidence and self-respect. I now feel like I can do anything, and at the age of 28, I feel like I'm just on the brink of my life, with so many options and desires for the years ahead of me. I imagine I'll always be in some kind of business for myself, but I'm not sure I ever want a retail operation again.

I am in the process of getting another business started, this time photography. This new situation seems to be ideal for my current lifestyle, as I can schedule my jobs according to whatever schedule Lonnie and I work out, with Kate, our baby, going to work with him. It's important to us that she be with us, and she's so independent and good that it's relatively easy for Lonnie to have her at his photo shop with him.

The type of photography I'm doing now is a photographic documentary service called Docu-Photo. I'll be photographing inside people's homes, their valuables, jewelry, etc., for insurance and safe-deposit purposes; real-estate photography; antique photography; inventory photography, etc. Since we already have good cameras and lenses, all I've had to invest in is a good lighting system and business cards, brochures, and stationery.

Beulah H. Schnadig

ANTIQUE DEALER AND APPRAISER,
El Paso, Texas.

Although a few of the women opened their business without previous experience, learned as they went along, and became financially successful, they found that even after eight years or longer, they still felt they did not know enough.

I feel that the more I learn, the less I know, and this isn't being said with humility because it sounds like a trite remark from a lot of people. However, it's true. In the beginning, when I went to do an appraisal, I did it with much more assurance than I'd do it now. Now I know how *much* there is to know and how *easy* it is to make a mistake. Let's say on furniture — is it original? or is it an 1800 copy of a 1700 piece of Queen Anne? or is it a piece that was manufactured this century? And you know, that really isn't easy. I see auctioneers and fine dealers make mistakes all the time. I'd rather say, "I don't know," or "I'm not sure," than spout something that sounds fantastically knowledgeable and isn't. That isn't to say that I don't know a great deal, because I feel I do.

In the 1950s my first husband and I drove up to Canada to attend a convention. There weren't many freeways and easy-access roads in those days, so we took back roads. In Canada, at that time, everybody's garage, everybody's barn, everybody's front yard was an antique shop. We stopped along the way and I started collecting. I really over-collected.

One day from the porch of our large Chicago home, I had a sale. I couldn't believe how people grabbed the things. Thereafter, we went to Canada every summer and we antiqued. The little business on the porch was with friends and neighbors only, and I didn't advertise. It was so much fun. If I made a dollar on an item, I was triumphant.

In 1965, three years after Bill's death, I married a man who was a consultant, but we had the time to do whatever we wanted. On our honeymoon, we headed for New York State, but along the way I said to Victor, "Come on. Let's go over into Canada." And we did. I dragged him into his first antique shop, and he really got the bug.

We collected and collected and collected and finally, having decided to do a show, we did an American Legion Flea Market, an indoor high-class one, not anything like the flea markets that I know about today. Our things were far superior to the other things there, so we made money, and we were terribly excited. Next, we got ourselves onto a Midwest antique circuit. We did the Hilton Hobby Show, one of the biggest in the country, and we had shows booked in Indianapolis and St. Louis, when Victor had a small stroke.

Since we considered leaving Chicago, I wrote to some of my childhood friends here in my native city of El Paso. One of them called us and said, "Beulah, if you really mean it, if you want a house where you can live and have your shop, I think we have it." We saw the house in July 1970, bought it a couple of months later, got here in October, and opened the shop on December first. Upstairs we converted the four bedrooms into a living room, dining room, den, and bedroom, and since there was already a second kitchen up there, we were totally self-sustained upstairs while the shop functioned downstairs.

Even though the overhead was quite negligible, we were in the red for about three years because we'd buy the things we liked. For the most part, the people in El Paso who came to us wanted primitives — butter churns, round oak tables, and so on. Although we prefer mahogany and walnut to oak, if I can lay my hands on what I really think is really good oak furniture, I'll buy it, because one learns to buy for one's market.

At first, because of Vic's special interest in napkin rings, we bought a great deal of American silver plate. Up until 1840, when the Smee battery was invented and electroplating was developed, only wealthy people could afford silver or Sheffield (a sheet of silver hand-rolled over copper). Now old Sheffield brings almost as much money as old silver. Literally hundreds of things hit the market with electroplating. We starting collecting things that made Mr. Average Man's table and home very exciting — including butter dishes, tilting ice water pitchers, and pickle jars.

Until Vic's recent very serious illness, we would go antiquing at the drop of a hat, to Ypsilanti, Michigan, or Chattanooga, Tennessee — anywhere we could buy well. Part of the marvelous bonus of being in this business is being able to go on buying trips that are legitimate. We've been to England, for example, seven or eight times. The only time I've taken a trip without Vic is when I flew to Chattanooga five years ago and couldn't buy one thing at the auction because, all of a sudden, the whole public had become fantastically aware of the fact that good antiques are probably as fine an investment as anything there is.

Buying anywhere but in El Paso is more fun because we're on a trip, but we've found that this town is quite loaded with things. Many of the earlier settlers had magnificent things brought from Europe or New York or Dallas. El Paso is a large army town — Fort Bliss and William Beaumont General Hospital are here, there are hundreds of retired colonels, and I myself know at least ten generals — and many retired military officers who come here move to smaller quarters and reduce their personal inventories. We just had an antique Japanese doll, for instance, which a high-ranking Japanese officer gave to an American general in Japan, who, in turn, gave it to a colonel who settled here in El Paso. He and his wife recently sold their house and had to get rid of many possessions, so they sold me the doll. It is now in a six-month layaway with someone from Big Spring, Texas.

A lot of times people want to sell me something and I'll say, "I don't think I can handle it with justice to you in El Paso. Let's write to Sotheby Parke-Bernet in New York" or to another fine auction house. Hanzel's in Chicago I would trust with my life. But many auc-

tion houses have shills in the audience. You just have to know with whom you're dealing. Over a period of time, you learn.

I love the decorum of the English auctions. There's no business of "Come on, pull up the price. It's worth this, it's worth that." It's incredible how some American auctioneers will play with you for an hour to get it up $2. In England, the auction hammer comes down and you're through and on to the next item. I like that because you have to make up your mind quickly how high you'll go, and once you're ready to bid, you bid — and, wow, you'd better bid in a hurry or it's gone. I get something called auction fever. I know I'm going to go, let's say, to $800, and pretty soon I'm at $1,100, and soon I'm at $1,200. I realize I have to stop, and I do sometimes. But sometimes I don't. I had a grandfather clock at one time that I just couldn't stop on. I finally got it, but it took me three years to sell it, and I made only a small profit. After three years, the market had changed.

We have many ordinary things in our shop, but predominantly we have good things that we feel are an investment and things that we believe in. We probably sell them under the market because dealers from out of town buy from us so frequently. One dealer from Houston flew here twice, spent $36,000, then sent two men by plane who rented the largest Hertz truck there is, packed here all day long, and drove back to Houston. Houston being the big, bustling city that it is, with a great deal of wealth, he must have done quite well with our things. I can't say that happens every day, but it's rewarding to know that some people do recognize the quality of what we have.

When Vic and I opened here eight and a half years ago, we sold things inexpensively, but when I went out to replace them — cut glass, for example — ha! I found I couldn't even buy them for what I'd sold them for. Today I'm paying probably two and three times as much to buy a good piece of cut glass as I sold it for when we opened. That could be an indication of what a good investment antiques are.

Collectibles today probably bring in as much as really fine antiques. It's incredible to me how some collectibles have soared in price. Goebel began putting out annual Hummel Christmas plates in 1971. I suspect that the first ones, which were probably issued in a limited edition because Goebel didn't know how they'd go, sold for $30. Would you believe I just had one come out of layaway here for $1,100? Last year, a lot of dealers were holding back with Hummels. There was a fight for power or control of who would be the distributor in this country. The 1978 Christmas plate came out at $65, then $75 — that was the manufacturer's price—but if you could get one for $200 you were lucky. A lot of dealers held on to maybe fifty. And you know what happened? Now the plates are down to $110. Those dealers held them too long. It's a crazy business, but I'd buy every old Hummel figurine I could lay my hands on for almost any price. People will come in here and ask for Hummels. They'll pass up a magnificent signed bronze, or a perfectly gorgeous piece of porcelain, for a Hummel figurine.

In the beginning, mostly older people came into the shop. Now young people are buying from me on layaway, knowing that they're getting something that will hold up. They're paying so much less than if they went and bought a new dining room set. I sold a beautiful overstuffed Queen Anne-style chair for $175 last week. If that couple could buy a similar chair for $600 or even anything where real wood shows today (furniture now has pleats of fabric coming down to conceal the poor-quality wood), they'd be lucky. This couple got a steal and they know it.

We aren't fly-by-night people, and yet as we've driven through cities and gone around the country, dealers have sold us things and not pointed out repairs or something wrong or have not told us the truth. To me, that's just about as bad as you can be. Because I'm going to tell you if there's a chip in a vase, I expect a person to tell me. But it's not so at all, and I should examine much more carefully. Actually, the only bad check we've ever taken was from another dealer. I don't understand this, because I feel that you must have integrity in order to have people respect you, in order for you to be able to live with yourself.

As I look back on the last twelve, thirteen years that we've been in business, it's amazing to me how much I've learned. My own expertise is probably mainly in silver and beautiful porcelain, but even so I find that I need to do a lot of study before I make blanket statements about certain things. As an English major in college, I learned where to go to get what I want to know. I think that has stood me in very good stead. On the other hand, when you can't find the information in one convenient place, you might wind up writing it yourself. My husband wrote a book on napkin rings because there were no sources. He studied social history and customs and manners and how the napkin ring evolved following the napkin. As we've always said,

"The fun is the search and the research."

I say to young people, or to anyone starting in the business: Step slowly and find out where your own interests and your own talents lie. Buy sagaciously if you can. This, I think, is very important. Also, don't go offering. I've learned this the hard way. If somebody has a little piece of pewter to sell, don't say, "All right, I'll give you $20." Say, "I don't offer. I never offer. Please tell me what you would like." Many times the person will say, "But I don't know what it's worth, and I know you'll be fair." It's very hard not to offer under those circumstances, but I've found that the minute a person gets a price from you, it's either a free appraisal or he'll say, "I'll think about it and I'll call ten other dealers." If he'll tell you what his price is, you either pay it or you don't. Or you say, "I really can't handle that," if you can't, "but I'll give you $15. I have to work with time in order to make a profit, and I have overhead, so if you want to keep that in mind, I'm good for that amount any time. I wish I could pay your price but you realize that, as a dealer, I can't."

If somebody says, "I want $15 for this," and you know it's worth $150, it's very tempting to buy it at $15, and I guess I have succumbed on occasion, but most of the time I'll say, "It's worth something more, and I'd rather pay you $40," or whatever. It makes me able to live with myself a little bit better.

Even though I'm supposedly semiretired, I've never worked harder — but I enjoy every second of it. There's a fantastic challenge in getting the merchandise. It *is* an addiction. I'm so crowded right now that it's crazy, and yet, if I had a call right now that sounded good, I'd just go flying.

In 1980, six months after we interviewed her, Beulah wrote:

As you know, Victor developed cancer in 1975. His was a valiant four-year struggle, but he passed away exactly a week after you had left El Paso. I am, of course, keeping up the business (which had been my full responsibility since his illness). I am fortunate to be happily occupied in a business lucrative enough for whatever my needs. Last year's gross was the best in nine years, and I count my business as a blessing, second only to the wonderful friends I have because of it.

Patricia M. Goffette

GENERAL CONTRACTOR,
Seattle, Washington.

Half of the 18 financially successful women we interviewed ($16,000 net and up) had several years of experience before engaging in their businesses. Pat had experience in speculative investments, and eventually she used her land investments as the "inventory" for her general contracting business.

I was in the stock market before I started building houses. I took $10,000 and put it in the stock market because that was a dream of mine, to buy and sell stocks on a speculative basis, not as long-term investments. I also went into futures on pork bellies, corn, cocoa beans, grain, and sugar, but I didn't like that, because after I bought something, the value wasn't always there. Sometimes it would go below what I paid for it, and I guess that's just against my feeling of a sound purchase. So after I was in it for about a year and a half, I took my money back out, and with the profits my husband, Jack, and I built a commercial building, which we felt was a much sounder investment. The value keeps going up, and it produces a steady income. I'm not concerned day to day what that building is worth, whereas in the stock market and the commodities, I never knew from one hour to the next exactly how much money I had left.

We didn't start out with very much. Jack was in the laundry business, and after we were married we moved into a small rental home he owned worth about $10,000. We spent four months fixing it up because the renters had completely destroyed it. After we renovated our home, we decided we wanted to make money, so we read a lot of books on how other people had done so. All the books advised how to make money after the first $75,000, but we were more concerned about what to do to get from zero to $40,000. We decided to start a program of investments and allot so much a month to payments, so we would start to build an equity and a net worth one step at a time.

We also decided to sell my MG sports car and use the money to make a down payment on a piece of property close to the Canadian border. Although we achieved an income of only $10 a month on the first piece of property, we developed that into buying and selling, on an average, one piece of property a month. We bought vacant land and didn't construct anything on it, but we developed experience in buying land. There's much to watch out for. Since I don't develop lots but buy already existing buildable lots, I have to know whether a property is in an older tract, whether it has a sewer, whether it will perk for a septic tank, and whether water and power are available. Usually there are homes built on many of the lots surrounding the one I'm looking at. I want to know why that lot is sitting there. Is something wrong with it? New lots today have much more engineering done on them, and of course all utilities are available and easily verified.

Beyond my experience in buying and selling land for our personal investments, I have a degree in finance with a minor in accounting, and all my 18 years of working experience has been in construction or construction-related firms. At one point, I took care of 18 different sets of books for a large construction company. Each investment, set up as a company, contained seven or eight apartment houses which I ran. Managers in the buildings solved all the small problems, but when they got to something they couldn't handle, they'd come to me and I'd sort it out. I did the advertising, all the remodeling, redecorating, and the color selection, and I collected the rents. I was a trouble shooter for the owner.

After that, I worked for a soils engineer, which gave me a good awareness of problems in soil testing and the staking of lots and elevations. Then in my last job, working for a home builder for about six years, I ran a one-girl office. I did everything from answering the phone to all of the bookwork and taxes, except for the corporate income tax; I picked out all the siding and the colors and decorated the insides of the houses.

I got tired of working for somebody else, and after lying back for a year I got fidgety and in 1974 decided I'd like to build homes—which had been in my mind for a good number of years. I started out to build one or two as a hobby, just something to keep me busy. The first day I went out, I bought two lots that I thought were very good, and even though I asked Jack's opinion and he approved, it was a little scary buying $24,000 worth of land.

At first I built one house at a time, and later I started two. I'd get one half-finished and start the second. Right now I have five going and will probably be starting another one in a few weeks, so that's six houses plus a remodeling at a main shopping center.

I don't buy the cheapest lots I can find. I've paid as little as $8,300, which is not cheap, and as much as $26,000, depending on the location and the view of Puget Sound. I also have some lots that I haven't sold yet which are valued at $40,000. I keep an inventory of lots to build on.

Before I buy any lot or sign over any earnest money, I go over a checklist. Then I go down and ask the city Planning Department, the Building Department, and the Department of Public Works, "What do you think? What are the restrictions?" They are very helpful. I've run into lots that seemed like super buys but then found out such things as that because of restrictions the house would have to be built below the driveway curb cut. I also go to the Utilities Department and check to make sure that the sewer and water are there and the power is available. Once I've determined that the restrictions won't prohibit my building a desirable house, I draw up the plot plans, submit them, and apply for a building permit. If something comes up while the plan is being reviewed, I go down and discuss it and make any necessary adjustments. Sometimes I've got to put in a street, or something like that, in order to get a permit. I comply with any rules and regulations.

I started out as a speculative builder. I'd partly finish a house, put in on the market, and see if somebody wanted it. Every one of them sold before I finished it. After that, people followed me and asked me to build custom on their lots, so now I'm about half and half.

Many people just assume that a lot is always buildable. Some people buy lots that are very wet and have had to put in special drains to control the pressure and the water flow so that it won't disturb the house.

I can build a fairly simple home in about three to three and a half months. The bigger homes take four to four and a half months, barring any unforeseen work stoppages or delays in getting materials. I make a rough design and then I have an architect draw them for structure and stress and proper planning. Architects come in with good ideas. We weigh them and decide what is and what isn't the best thing to do for the lot, the location, and the view.

I subcontract out almost everything. I hire heavy equipment to dig the hole, a crew to put the foundation in, framers to frame the house, and roofers to put the roof on, on a per-job basis. My secretary, foreman, and a couple of carpenters do all the things that can't be subcontracted out.

Some of the finish work I do myself with my own employees, and I train people to do the custom work. I stand over them and say, "Take one step at a time. First do this," then I come back and say, "All right, now that we've got that accomplished, this is the next step," and we proceed step by step. It's not only physically tiring, it's mentally exhausting. I have to stay one step ahead of everyone and make sure that the jobs are done the way I've asked. But, as a result of my careful supervision, a number of customers have come to me and said, "We've been following you around for about a year, looking at your homes, and we want you to build our new home." That's a feather in my cap, and I'm very conscious of protecting that image. I'm welcome in the homes of all the people I've sold to. We are friends. I see them in the grocery store. I live in the same neighborhood. The financial rewards come because I'm conscientious.

My homes have four, five, or six bedrooms, family rooms off the kitchen, and large hallways no less than 4 feet wide so that they can be used as galleries. I include such amenities as tinted windows and insulated windows, parquet floors, better than baseline brick and stone, special trawlings on the walls, hand-routed woodwork which is all hand finished, personalized showers, instant hot water, microwave ovens, trash compactors, griddles and grills, and all the other deluxe things that people dream about and want in their homes. We put in electronic air filters and built-in vacuum cleaner systems. We put in ample outlets and lighting. We custom-design the fireplaces and have custom-made railings for our stairwells. We do things a lot of other builders don't do. My least expensive home is $85,000, and they go up to the $200,000 price range.

I've got two strikes against me. I'm not only a woman contractor, I'm a Polish woman contractor. Everybody teases me about that. So far I haven't built any houses upside down.

A year later, Pat wrote:

I now have 11 jobs and a 16-unit apartment-townhouse-style complex going. I have my own foundation company now, have added one more gal to the office, got another van, and now have a total of ten employees. It's lots of fun and lots of work.

Stella McBride, C.M.*

CONSULTANT, HOME AND BUSINESS ORGANIZER,
Denver, Colorado.

All the women we interviewed who were financially successful worked within specific time frames with specific plans and deadlines for what they needed to accomplish each day as well as specific objectives set for the more distant future. All but two of these women had delineated space for each specific function of the business. Stella specializes in providing techniques to facilitate everyday achievement through efficient space organization.

I was working at the University of California Medical Center in San Francisco as an administrator, and someone said I had unique skills and should start my own business. So I started thinking about it, and when I moved to Denver, I thought, "This is a good opportunity." When I was ready to open, I called the TV station and said, "I'm starting an unusual business," and they put me on Channel 9 news. About three weeks later I had an article in *University Park News* and then another article in the *Jewish News*. My first clients called because of the articles and because of seeing me on TV.

*C.M. — Certified Manager

Helping people make order out of chaos is an unusual profession. People are often deeply ashamed of the chaos that they wrought — mostly by themselves, but occasionally by someone else. Putting things in order is very simple, but helping someone learn how to keep order and how to live with it and work with it is a tremendous challenge. There is no usual way of doing this. That is the great challenge —that each assignment has almost no relationship with any other because what is in sequence for me may not be for someone else.

I suggest that the objectives be identified: What is wanted? When is it wanted, how often is it going to be wanted, and who is going to want it? You or someone else? Depending on what we're talking about, it's then put in sequence of being wanted, in a shape or format or color that is recognizable to the person who's going to be using it so that it's retrievable. The point is not to put things away, it's how to get things back once they're put away. Thus it's entirely the skill of retrieval.

People are terrified. They want to hold on to the old way of doing things, and they sometimes enjoy their problems. The clients I enjoy the most, really, are the ones who are able to convince themselves that they want to make a change. I've refused projects where I think the clients just pretend to be working toward the objective but in fact are not doing it. Also, unless they're willing to make a certain amount of commitment, I advise them that the project won't be successful. When someone *really* wants to get something together and get organized, I can help because I have the skills — maybe some tricks, but mainly just the basic knowledge of where to start and how to do it.

For instance, a kitchen may need additional shelving or Rubbermaid aids in the cabinets to increase the space. Often a kitchen is stuffed with things that are seldom used and that the client doesn't want to throw out. Sometimes I find that everything is as far as possible from its place of use. I go cabinet by cabinet. When did you use this last? When did you look at this last? When did you touch this last? My objective is to get things that are never or rarely used, boxed and put in storage. Most kitchens are fine, and there would be plenty of space if they weren't filled up, for example, with things given to women by their mother-in-law that they won't throw away and yet that are taking all the prime space. I think that's the biggest problem.

I go back and visit. Some revert to their old habits, but if they really want to get organized and keep things tidy in order to save time from looking and running around, they maintain order pretty well. I think most people want to get organized. Women in their homes need their time more and more, as do other members of the family, and very often there's pressure created because of the lack of organization. Then family members have problems with themselves because frequently they're looking for something, can't find it, and therefore they're running late.

It takes a lot of motivation to organize seriously and not just say, "Oh, I'll have an organizer come in, and we'll pay her, and we'll let her do it." I think the first thing that happens is that they realize I'm not going to do it all. I'm going to teach *them* how to do it. It would probably be more lucrative for me to do it and keep coming back like a maid, but I don't think it's constructive, and therefore I don't advocate it. Teaching people to change habits and ways of thinking is quite difficult unless they really decide they want it, and when they do, it is just fascinating and really enjoyable. I think people do need help, and there's no shame in needing assistance. I need assistance in many ways and call people who help me.

I started out working with home organization, and my work evolved into business organization in Denver and elsewhere. Now I'm doing three types of work: business and institutional organization, working with individuals in their homes, and assisting others who come to Denver to consult with me to start similar businesses.

At the University of Alaska, I worked for the newly established Office of the Dean of the College of Environmental Sciences to establish comprehensive research and organizational files. Through the use of color, I instituted a system whereby various research projects could be distinguished and retrieved. After the assignment was completed, the dean wrote me a reference letter stating that "the files, indeed, are now a useful and not terminal repository of information."

I was hired as a consultant to a large law firm for several months to reorganize records and organize descriptions of jobs and the accountability for who does what type of work. Originally a staff of five or six covered file retrieval, processing and delivering mail, running errands to court or clients, and miscellaneous clerical functions. After a specific job accountability system was set up and implemented, each person understood his or her job responsibility and could be proud of accomplishments in a specific area, and it worked more effectively for the firm.

A large part of my work consists of setting up "employee accountability systems" — organizing jobs so that employees understand what they are doing and are motivated to excel rather than be in a state of confusion and not know what is expected of them. This type of work interests me as much as retrieving things in homes or in offices. Again it's categorizing. I may not have eliminated a function, but I may have switched it or regrouped it. A lot of people are very bored and unhappy in their work because they don't understand what's going on, why they're doing it, and what it's connected to. They don't know what's expected of them. Their job has not been clearly delineated and communicated.

When I go to a client, I talk about ultimate goals. I basically reorganize job structures — that is, who does what. The client and I work on it together, and then I finalize it and present it for approval.

I've done hiring, evaluation, termination, purchasing, and any number of other functions for a client. I found I could make more money if I sold equipment, but I think that is a conflict of interest, and I choose to provide only a service instead of trying to push a specific manufacturer's product. I recommend and do some purchasing if clients want me to, but I am free to recommend any product or supplier.

I'm in favor of tremendous simplicity. I think we clutter our lives and make things very complicated, and so a lot of my work is just simply making things simpler to deal with. I believe a business should be run in a businesslike fashion no matter where it is conducted. If it's conducted from a home, delineating office space is almost essential, and keeping business life, finances, and records separate *is* essential. The number of businesses that start with money coming into a private account and without a set of books is amazing. One of the things that I help people with is teaching them to be professional.

Some men and women who have businesses in their homes think that business rules do not apply to them, that they are exempt from the business plan or from the creation of a business identity, or sometimes from behaving in a businesslike manner toward clients or customers. They believe that being homey and folksy and friendly is going to win the day. Although being friendly is essential, to give people confidence it's still very important that you are organized and operating professionally. You need to have professional and businesslike pride. Your business affairs should not be chaotic and sloppy. It isn't enough to have a skill or a product unless you also know how to promote it and yourself in an appropriate and businesslike manner. Women would be a lot more successful in selling their wares or their crafts if they organized and structured their businesses and joined business associations such as the Chamber of Commerce or the National Management Association — organizations that are acceptable entities in the business world.

When people go into their own businesses, they think, "Now I can set my own hours," or they think that they can work or take off time when they want to, but usually a business requires a lot of time. It is a fallacy to think that when you are in business for yourself, in your own home, you set your hours. In consulting work, your clients will predetermine your hours, and your hours are likely to be far longer than working at a regular job. When you have your own business, there is always something to be done — especially if you are conducting a service or creating a product yourself, as well as keeping books and analyzing legal and financial reports and records.

In many ways it is far more satisfying for people to work for themselves and be their own boss, but they tend to find out that they themselves are the toughest boss they've ever had.

Two years later, Stella wrote us:

I continue to be very busy. I went to the Netherlands to work on sorting out the legal files and personal documents for a private law practice. Most of the material I was handling was in English and there were many interesting old documents which related to World War II and the rights of Dutch citizens during that period. I assisted in determining what might be of value to the Netherlands War Institute and what should be saved from a legal or personal point of view.

I'm working on two home organization projects and two different projects at the Adolph Coors Company: one at the Brewery and one at the Construction Division. Both involve record management and systems analysis of the records. Since "records" do not do anything by themselves, this involves people, and each department is unique. The people, the objectives, and functions are so different. A woman from Houston wishes to start her own business there and is coming the end of April for a ten-hour training session on "the joys and pit-falls" of this unique type of business.

I recently became a member of the National Association of Parliamentarians as well as of the Colorado Association of Parliamentarians. I am developing a workshop on How To Be a Professional, and I spoke on Organization for the Working Woman to the American Association of Business Women. So you can see my business continues to be multifaceted and challenging.

*For information write: Stella McBride, C.M., Organization Plus, 1330 Rosemary Street, Denver, Colorado 80220.

Gail A. Kiesler

DESIGNER AND FABRICATOR OF THREE-DIMENSIONAL
QUILTS AND WALL HANGINGS,
Stowe Hollow, Vermont.

Financial success is not the primary objective of some of the women. Gail's quilts sell for more than $1,000 each, she's two years behind in back orders, and her customers are willing to wait as long as it takes just to have one of her creations. Still, money is not her motive for engaging in her craft business.

This business is fun for me. I started it for fun and I'll end it when it isn't fun. If I had to support my family, I could go the commercial route and get the ideas and just design. I know I could make a darn good living that way, but it would be no fun for me. It's not the way I work.

Often the women have widely diverse talents and their home business permits them to make use of all of them.

The first Vermont Village quilt that I made was flat, and I thought, "Uh huh. Pop it up!" and so then you get the gravestones all standing up and a row of flowers, the real estate office, the cars, and that sort of thing. That's the fun. Often I have painted with acrylic paints that can go into the washing machine, too, and then embroidered and then appliqued and then maybe added some soft

sculpture. Sometimes I use a wood backing to give it dimension—whatever works.

The construction of three-dimensional quilts depends on a
mechanical sense, basically. I look at something and I know how it
functions. You give me something and I can take it apart and put it
together. I can do that in fabric, too. Some of it is just innate, I guess,
because people ask, "Where do you get your patterns for all of
these?" They just don't think people make things without a pattern.
*When the home environment can be controlled and interruptions cut
to a minimum, the creative process can be totally absorbing.*

My mind is on the job that I'm doing for the moment. I couldn't
function if I looked at the list of things that I have to do in the next
year or two. I never know what day it is. I'm lucky if I know what
month it is. I'm oblivious to what happens outside. Lou will come
home and ask, "What's the weather forecast for tomorrow?" I don't
know even what it's been today, because I'm up in my little hole doing my thing.

I was new in town and didn't know anyone. The kids were in a
cooperative nursery school where the parents assist. At the first fund-
raising meeting for our bazaar, I thought, "Maybe they could raffle off
a quilt." I had been an art major at school and had always sewn, and
I had quilt in the car, one I had made for the kids' beds, and I
brought it into the meeting. Everybody oo'd and ah'd and said, "Oh,
yeah. We'd really like this." That year we made four times as much
money for the nursery school than had been made for the whole
prior year. For three years after that we raffled off a quilt I made, and
each year we printed more tickets.

I had had enough response from the raffle to try the Stowe Craft
Show. I figured, what could I lose? Whatever didn't sell I could
always use for wall hangings here at home. For the first craft show, I
had my three-dimensional Vermont Village Quilt, five or six other
quilts ranging from double to queen size, and six or eight baby quilts,
as well as wooden puzzles and appliquéd bags.

The response was excellent. I didn't have much that was unsold.
People ordered things there, and soon they were telling their friends
and they were calling me up. I still have people four years later who
had taken my little card and are calling me from the Midwest and
West saying, "We would love one of your quilts." After the fair, I

took a couple of big quilts that weren't sold to the State Craft Center in Middlebury. You have to be juried to be on display at the Craft Center, and when I walked into the room and opened my garbage bag with the quilts, the lady said, "Ahhh! These are terrific. We want them all." I left things there, and that's what got me rolling. I haven't done the Stowe fair in the last two years because I have too many special orders. I had to whip everything out of the State Craft Center for the shop when we opened last year in June.

The shop came about when several artists got together to sell their work. They decided that works in certain media display better in contrast to pieces in other media, and they asked me if I would like to join them for a year's trial. I was flattered, since they're all good craftsmen, but I really didn't know whether I should pay out X dollars in rent that I didn't really have to be paying. As it happens, although I've been the one who's earned the most money down there, it's nice to work with people whose interests are similar.

The craft shop is a six-way partnership. We split rent and expenses. Each of us works one day every six days in the shop, and the shop is open seven days a week. The nice thing about the shop is that each of us can do something, so we're not just sitting on our butts all day, and people see us working. I sit there and zig-zag for eight hours. We get together about once a month to discuss everything from how the shop looks to where do we go from here to what type of things we're turning out. The more I talk with men in the craft industry, the more I feel there is far less chauvinism in this field than in others. Men who do something with their hands appreciate women who are making their living at that sort of thing. It's probably the first time since college that I've been really good friends within a male/female relationship without having some sort of sex attitude.

All sorts of customers come in who really take their time and look at our things and appreciate them and ask questions about the work. They're interested in what we're doing and how things are made. Also, I enjoy it when people say, "Boy, I can't afford anything right now, but you have terrific things here. We really *like* what you're do-ing.."

I've got two years' worth of orders. I could sign up for the rest of my life. One lady visiting the shop while I was working there didn't realize it was my portfolio she was leafing through, and she looked at my little note about not being able to take any more orders. She said,

"Well, how old is this person? Does she think she's going to die before she gets them done?" "Well," I said, "It could get to that point." I don't know if I want to be making quilts two years down the road. Maybe I want to be doing something else.

I always think, "Well, I can squeeze one more in"—like my last project. People who were opening a new restaurant in Burlington called up and said, "Gail, we know you're really busy, but we'd love to have a wall hanging for over the salad bar for the restaurant." I always think a wall hanging is like 36" x 24" so I said, "Oh, sure, I can work that right in." It was right before we were going on vacation, so I ended up making a windjammer and waves and three-dimensional sea gulls that hang all over the place, and again shoving back some other orders that I'd obviously gotten before they ever ordered that, but that was totally because I figured, "A wall hanging—I can whip that out in between other things."

Then there's a lady here in Stowe who is building a new home, and she wants quilts in every room. The house started out with four bedrooms, and now they're having nine. That will take me a year, at any rate, if I'm to do stuff for the shop with it. It's not that I don't want to do it. It's just physically, what can I do? I'm one person, and I do work 12 hours a day, more or less, seven days a week *because* I love it, not for any other reason. I try to get in as much as I can. If I really like the people and they really like my stuff, that gets me going, too.

People are always asking, "How much time would that quilt there take?" I've only made one quilt from start to finish, Boom! That was for the Stowe winter carnival two years ago. They wanted one for the cover of their brochure, and, again, we were going on vacation in six days, so I worked day and night on that and finished it in one fell swoop. Usually I'll stop in the middle and start on another if I get a great idea. That's what keeps me going. The ideas are the fun part. If a color excites me or an idea excites me, I cut it out and see what happens, because it's an evolutionary process.

For instance, the director of the Frog Hollow Craft Center wanted a quilt for her parents, who live in Connecticut on an old farm. She said, "It's near the shore." I started one with shoreline but then went out to sea. It turned into a seascape versus a landscape, with a shoreline so it no longer fills the function that I started with and no longer fills the order. Now I have to start again. That's what I mean when things evolve. I don't quite know where I'm going.

The fun is in the doing for me, and once I've done it, that's the end of it for me. I hate to duplicate things. I have duplicated small Jack and the Beanstalk baby quilts because people just love that so. Not one person who bought it has kids. One couple in their seventies bought it for their condominium. The fun is also having other people enjoy them, like my village quilt, which is in the State Craft Center's permanent collection after having also gone to Switzerland.

My fantasy would be to have a gigantic building where, when I wanted to sew, I'd have my sewing corner, and then I would move down to where I could weave, and then I would go to where I could paint, and then I'd have somebody clean up after me. When I used to sew clothes for myself, I would, as often as not, not do it just because I had to go through the mechanics of getting things out and cleaning up. The cleaning up would get me, or I shoved it down the table and got dinner ready around that. Now it's delightful that I can just go up to my own workspace and be as messy as possible. I let only certain people into my sewing room. I have to know them well. They had a list in a lady's magazine that said a good friend is one that you'd let clean out your drawers after you died. I figured a good friend was one that I'd let up in my sewing room, because then they know the real me. I have nothing left to hide.

My parents-in-law have always been very proud of what I do. Louie's father is one of those that gives a house tour, and he took friends of his on a tour of our house. After they saw my sewing room, the wife said, "Oh, Gail! Thank you! For 25 years I've been telling my husband, this is the way I want to work. Now I have to get everything out and put everything away." And he said, "Gail, you've just convinced me that something *can* be made out of chaos."

Maggie Weisberg

VICE-PRESIDENT OF TWO INVENTORS' ORGANIZATIONS
AND EDITOR OF AN INVENTORS' NEWSLETTER, *
Tarzana, California.

Home business owners start at home for any number of reasons, not the least of which is to take care of a loved one. Maggie Weisberg began working from home first so she could care for her sick father and later because of a sick husband (who died five months after our interview with her). Similar tragedies occurred in the lives of other women, and they revealed how their home businesses softened the sharp edges of grief and provided necessary income, continued involvement, and comfort. Inventing, by its very nature, is a creative and compelling endeavor, charging those individuals involved in it with enthusiasm and vitality. We asked Maggie, Who are the inventors?

All of us are inventors, in one form or another. And we come with varying talents, intensity, capability, and dedication.

There isn't any one type of person who comes into Inventors Workshop International (IWI). Two weeks ago a short, fairly nice-

*The Lightbulb, P.O. Box 251, Tarzana, California 91356. One-year subscription, $24.00.

looking man came into our office. He didn't communicate very well until he started talking about his invention; then there was no stopping him. He just poured forth the words. He had never married. He had never dated. In a small apartment he lives the life of a hermit and a recluse. He goes to his job, he comes home, and he invents. That is all he loves. That is all he wants.

Some people invent because the drive inside is so strong. One very wealthy inventor is a religious man, and he feels that ideas come to him from God. He wakes up in the middle of the night, and the ideas come so fast he cannot write them down fast enough. In 1975, from about 600 ideas, all of which he thought were viable and good, he selected 117 inventions that he felt had the most potential for gain, for profit, for worth to people, and he applied for patents on them.

When I first came to IWI in 1971, the inventions that filtered in from women seemed rather simplistic — not insignificant, because everything has its own worth, but none in the technical field. For so many years, women had been discouraged from entering any areas of study that were considered men's province. Only the fields that surround the home, child care, home economics, typing, and the very subordinate positions in industry seemed open to them; this was their place, and they had not tried to enter schools of engineering or architecture. Their inventions reflected that shortcoming. Now more and more women enter technical fields, and even construction, and I believe we will soon experience a tremendous revolution in our technology because we have a more balanced input.

I give women exactly the same advice that I would to a man: "Encourage this gift of creativity." When one idea comes and it is stifled, a second idea comes a little slower. If you continue to stifle creativity, pretty soon it simply dies from lack of nourishment. I think in order to develop it — in order for it to become so much a part of you that you cannot help but be creative at everything you do — you must encourage that self inside. You must be true to yourself regardless of others or other things.

We lived in Hungary and owned some property near the railroad that was coveted by the conquerers who had taken over that part of the country. They tried to simply move in, and my parents fought back. Then one night they took my father away and beat him senseless and two weeks later dropped him on the stoop. His flesh was morbid — absolutely black. When he recovered, six months later, Mother and Dad simply took a bed sheet, literally poured as many belongings into it as they could, and tied the four ends together. Under cover of night we traveled to Bucharest, and left by ship for America.

When we landed in New York on July 4th, great fireworks greeted us. We decided that America was the most beautiful country in the world. What other country would open its heart to immigrants so generously? We couldn't land at once, of course, and when we finally debarked on the 5th, we learned that they were not celebrating our coming after all. But it was still a marvelous feeling to arrive here. There were five of us. I had two brothers, 8½ and 12, and I was 5½. Father was 40 and Mother was 30.

I never realized what a traumatic experience it must have been to be so totally uprooted until recently someone pointed out to me that I don't remember a thing that happened prior to the age of 5½. In Hungary we had had a lovely home, and I had had a governess. When we came here, we had nothing.

I grew up in California and married, and for many years I worked as an American Bar Association liaison representative to the television and movie industry. Writers call the ABA if their script has something to do with the courts — for instance, who's present at a particular type of hearing and what the purpose of the hearing is. By osmosis I have learned a great deal about law.

Some seven years ago, I suddenly decided I was an inventor. I came up with a couple of ideas that I thought were good, and I didn't know what to do about them. I heard an advertisement on the radio promoting a company that helped inventors like myself fabricate and market their inventions, so I went to see the company. The suite was very large with several offices. I told the young man who greeted me about my idea, and he said he thought it was marvelous. "I'll tell you what," he said. "I want to consult with our manager. Let's see what he says about something I have in mind."

When he came back, he said, "He confirms what I believe, which is that you have a great idea with a lot of potential. Actually," he went on, "we usually charge about $3,500 for getting a product on the market, but because we believe your idea has such great promise, we're willing to forego half of that. We'll put up half if you'll put up the other half."

I left there not feeling very happy. I didn't really think that was the way inventions should go. I did nothing for another two or three months, and then I heard a public service announcement about a workshop that helped inventors and guided them. My husband, my business partner, and I went to one of their chapter meetings in the West Valley. There was Mel Fuller, sitting with one other workshop member in a fairly dark little room. Before we left, all three of us had signed up. We were impressed by Mel's sincerity, his struggle, and his obvious desire to help inventors.

Mel was an inventor himself who had been ripped off by the type of company that I had first visited. He had also worked for a large corporation that demanded he sign over his patent to them in return for $1 and continued employment. He needed the employment, so he signed the release, but he was so incensed that he still has that $1 check framed in his office to remind him of the need of individual inventors for a protective umbrella organization. That particular invention was the freeze-frame action, which you now see on television all the time. It's used throughout the industry.

Inventions are risky. You're never quite sure, no matter how good the idea is, whether it's before its time, whether it'll go over, or how it'll be accepted by consumers. It's tough to gamble everything you have on an invention.

Besides, companies are extremely reluctant to pay royalties, and the Justice Department seems to regard patents as a monopoly to be treated with hostility. Actually, America's founding fathers saw such a tremendous need for patents for the growth and development of this country that they inserted a separate section into the Constitution about the need to protect inventors and to give them a limited period of exclusivity in which they can *benefit* and derive the fruits of their efforts.

When a patent is challenged in court, often the case is heard by a judge who knows nothing about the process of inventing or patenting. As a result, over 50% of the patents are invalidated. In 1978, our own Ninth Circuit Appellate Court here in California invalidated over 87% of the patents that came before it. The cost of filing for a patent, including filing fees and attorneys' fees, ranges from $1,500 to $5,000 — and that's a lot of money for an individual to have to come up with, only to have one branch of the government invalidate what another branch has granted.

The key word in patent law is *obviousness*. An extremely well-done invention is a very simple invention. Simplicity is often misconstrued by the judge as obviousness. He is likely to say, "This is obvious; therefore it cannot be protected. You're not entitled to 17 years of exclusivity on this invention."

In order to prevent judges from confusing simplicity with obviousness we at Inventor's Workshop encourage every member who comes to us to invest in an inventor's journal, a bound book with ruled, numbered pages, so that the inventor can record his progress on his invention from concept to completion — the changes, expenses, the list of people he has shown it to, etc. *Everything* is recorded so that should his invention and patent be challenged, he'll have a record of the work that went into the invention to show it wasn't obvious at all.

It shocked me to realize that while one of the tasks of a corporate attorney is to protect the patents claimed by his own company, another task is to break the patents on products that are brought to the company. It's ridiculous. I don't think there is enough that we can do to protect our inventors.

Anyway, I had some time on my hands, so I went to see Mel and Louise Fuller and ask them if they could use any public relations. I was very upset by the fact that such a worthwhile effort was growing so slowly. I thought that, with a few well-directed letters, we could possibly achieve some income other than having to depend solely on membership growth to provide funds. Before I knew it, I found myself more and more involved with the Workshop until now, from my home, I'm devoting full time to it.

We have worked together — without pay — feeding the kitty to keep it moving and to keep the postage and other expenses paid.

Mel paints on an extremely broad canvas. His vision is to have an Inventor's Trade Center in Ventura where people from all over the world — industrialists, small business people, etc. — can come at their convenience to browse through the permanent displays to find and buy or license a product or display their own products for market testing.

As more and more needs of the inventors surface, services have to be created. Since inventors needed to expose their products to the public and the business community, we initiated an annual Inventors Exposition. Then we noticed that, despite the fact that most of our exhibitors had dozens of cards from business people expressing interest in their products, only two or three out of 100 succeeded in consummating a licensing agreement. We decided that the inventor needed an agent to represent him, so we formed Inventors Licensing and Marketing Agency. We also decided that in order to keep ourselves totally separated in concept and in activity from the front money organizations, we would not charge for our services until we succeeded. This has meant that during the first three years we virtually, have been paying for the privilege of serving inventors.

So now we have two organizations, Inventors Workshop International,.which is a nonprofit organization, and Inventors Licensing and Marketing Agency (ILMA), a profit organization. IWI functions on three levels:

1. It provides an invention evaluation service for its members which gives an inventor a written report on the feasibility, protection, development, manufacturing, and marketing of his or her invention.

2. It takes an advocacy position to promote the protection of inventors, such as supporting the creation of an Office of Patent Prosecutor whose responsibility it would be to enforce the right authority granted under the patent. The goal is to provide internal balance to the Justice Department's anti-trust attitude toward patents and to bring patent theft under criminal law.

3. It supports individual inventors through education and association through chapter meetings.

ILMA, the spin-off organization, has been in existence since 1976. It has been a struggle to get ourselves established but we kept at it until we evolved an effective marketing method.

Our first catalog of ILMA Products Available for Sale or Licensing, issued in 1977, consisted of just several stapled sheets. Our second catalog, issued in 1978, was a compendium of about 200 products bound in one volume. We printed 500, and the question remained, How to get them to the right people?

We put a small ad into the *Wall Street Journal* stating that the catalog was available. We were stunned by the number of huge companies that responded. Our catalog found its way overseas— to Europe, to Asia, and to the Middle East — and suddenly we are receiving inquiries from all over the world about our products. We are no longer approaching individual manufacturers; *they* are approaching us. They have looked through the catalog and seen something that fits in their product line, and they're writing us. It's a totally different ball game.

Some large corporations that have subscribed to our catalog have undoubtedly ordered it so they could simply turn it over to their research and development departments, which, in turn, would look at it and then simply invent around whatever idea appealed to them. But inventors must subject themselves to this in order to get their inventions considered.

Unfortunately, over years of being ripped off, some inventors have become paranoid: "I've got the greatest invention in the world. The whole world is waiting, but I can't show it to you because you'll steal it." We have to take a chance. However, the fact that a group like Inventors Workshop exists gives hope to inventors all over the world. Beyond IWI, I would like to see schools offer courses teaching young people to create. There *is* a formula. There is a series of steps that must be taken to bring an idea to fruition.

There are so many areas that we have not yet been able to touch because of lack of time and money and staff. But we are getting there. In the process of growth and development in any area—whether it's a physical project, or spiritual development, or expertise in a sport — development comes in spurts. A very sharp rise is followed by a leveling off. During the leveling-off period we assimilate what we have learned, and sometimes we stay on that level so long that we become despondent. But then, after we've assimilated and we're ready, up we spurt again. Growth is never a straight climb uphill. It's level, it's up, it's level, it's up, it's level, it's up. The leveling-off periods are necessary to future growth. That's where Inventors Workshop is now. Without the leveling off, we wouldn't have a strong foundation. We've spent most of the eight years since starting IWI building a foundation. Very little has been seen above ground. Now we're becoming visible.

June Harrison

OWNER OF HOME ANSWERING SERVICE,
Palatine, Illinois.

Fifteen of the women we interviewed worked from home because they had to. They couldn't afford day care for their children, they needed to take care of a sick or disabled loved one, they were too sick themselves, or they couldn't get comparable jobs outside their homes which paid as much as they could make through their own home businesses. In 1979, June Harrison was netting over $31,000 from her home answering service which she started in April 1968.

My husband was ill for 12 years before he died, and it became necessary with nine children to provide the living. To begin with, I took in ironing and did babysitting. I put up a sign in the supermarket, but one day someone from the state picked up the card and said I had to quit because I wasn't licensed and I had too many children of my own to get a license. I could provide care for only about four children, and four wasn't enough for me to make a living. One of my babysitting customers knew I was home all day, and since he was having a little problem with one of his employees, he wanted to know if I would answer his phone. Another parent whose daughter I had taken care of needed an answering service, too, so I just hung two phones on the wall.

I called a woman in town who had another small answering service on a 9-to-5 basis and who wanted only 20 phones. Since she began sending me anybody she couldn't handle, I asked her if I could come and see what she had and how she was doing it. When I went over there, she told me how she answered them, but she wouldn't give me any other advice, so I went home and tried to figure out just what I could do. My daughter Mary Ellen was enrolled in the work/study program at the high school and since the school agreed that she could work with me, Mary Ellen and I really started the business together. She worked with me until she graduated.

I wasn't able to get into the Yellow Pages because I had just missed the printing, so I had to start without that help. But gradually I built up to nine phones. Meanwhile, I was still babysitting and taking in laundry and hopping from phone to phone. Then a woman whose children I was taking care of and who worked for Illinois Bell said there was a definite need for a 24-hour answering service in Palatine, so I started such a service.

After I got to nine phones, I decided to get a "call director," which has 29 lines plus a personal line. I filled that, and when I had about 20 more. I thought I might as well take the next step and order a switchboard.

I had always managed to keep my bills paid, but I think the dear Lord above was with me, because Illinois Bell decided to take a risk and let me start the business. I had no start-up capital, but in order to lease the equipment, they required me to sign a five-year contract which held me liable for whatever number of months would be left should I decide to quit. Now I have two switchboards, and I'm considering a third. I have about 200 customers.

Two women operators work in the morning, and I rely on students in the high school work/study program in the afternoon. It helps them and it helps me, too. In the evening, my oldest daughter works from 6:00 to 11:00. I take the boards from 11:00 P.M. until 9:00 A.M. Sometimes I can sleep for two hours, and sometimes I'm up every half hour. It varies. Doctors get calls at all hours, and I have several trouble lines — the Bridge, a counseling organization mainly for teenagers; Crossroads Clinic, which counsels people on venereal disease, pregnancies, and abortions; and Alcoholics Anonymous.

And if a food-vending machine goes out of order at a hospital, I receive calls to inform a man on duty to go out to service it. I also call people who ask me to wake them.

Not all of my customers take the 24-hour service. I have one rate for five days a week, one for six, and one for seven. Customers get 75 calls for the monthly fee and then are charged 10¢ a call after that. I write an average of 8,000 messages a month, but we answer many more calls than that, because many people don't leave messages. I save the messages for three months. One client calls back constantly: "I lost the messages. Repeat them."

Because it's too difficult to get someone to work during the holidays, Christmas and Thanksgiving family dinners are held here. Six of my children plus a grandchild live in the house, and with the other three, their husbands, and their children, we have up to 40 people for the holidays. The switchboards aren't that busy, though, and we turn them up so we can hear any calls.

It's very hard to live and work in the same place. I get up, I go to work, I go to bed. It's confining. If I don't get out, I want to go up the wall. I began to drive about 18 months ago. I got angry one day because I couldn't do what I wanted to. I had seen an ad in the paper for a car, and my son-in-law checked it out and said, "If you don't buy it, I will," so I bought the car first and then took the driving test.

When my husband was alive, he would pick up the groceries. Afterward, it became part of the operators' job. I'd go to the store and get the groceries and then call them up to come and get me. One operator would take both positions for the ten minutes it took to get me. That was risky, because it seems if you step away, that's when those boards light up. Now I drive myself, and there's no problem. I also go ballroom dancing twice a week, take at least two days of exercise classes in the mornings, and one night of tap dancing a week.

I really like the business except for conflicts. One dentist, for instance, insisted that when he called up and we said he had no messages, he *did* have messages because so and so "said they called in!" That's one reason I keep the messages. I finally asked him, "Doctor, are you charging people for not canceling?" He *was* charging them, so I think the people were saying they called in when they didn't. I went down to the library and xeroxed the messages and sent them to him. I said that I was willing to stand behind any mistake that was made, but, by the same token, I wanted to be vindicated should it prove that I was right. I still have him as a customer.

- One thing I learned very quickly is that if a client has a problem, it is *that* person's problem. It isn't mine. Another woman who had an answering service in the area called to warn against my taking on a customer she was getting rid of because she didn't like the way he ran his business. She thought he was spending too much for advertising. She's no longer in business, and I've had him as a customer since I began. He runs a very successful business and he pays very promptly.

I consider myself extremely fortunate to have gotten into the answering service business because I've been able to provide for everybody. I'm hoping to continue as long as I'm capable. There's no forced retirement in this business.

Cynthia Paulis

HEAD HUNTER OF PHYSICIANS, NURSES, AND
ADMINISTRATORS FOR HOSPITALS AND COMMUNITIES,
Alexandria, Virginia.

*Age is often a contributing factor in the decision to start a home
business. The job market discriminates against the young as well as
the old.*

I built the program from nothing to something, but once it was
going full speed, despite my success, I was prevented from becoming
the director because, I was told, "Don't be ridiculous! You're too
young and female."

I have worked since I was 15, so I had to grow up very quickly. There
was a lot of responsibility placed on my shoulders. I didn't have the
time to sit and listen to the stereo. My father was very ill. There was
no one else at home — just my mother and myself, since my sister
was away at college. I had to assume a lot of roles and responsibilities, and I learned to be an adult at a very early age.

I majored in business at Georgetown University, studied business
management in Japan, and then got a master's degree in business
administration from George Washington University. After that, it was
quite simple. I had to pay the rent, so I got a "head hunting" job. The

company I worked for put me in charge of recruiting osteopathic physicians for hospitals, especially in rural communities in the Middle West. That had never been done before, so we had to sell the hospital boards and administrators on hiring us to do the search for them. I built the program from nothing to something, but once it was going full speed, despite my success, I was prevented from becoming the director because, I was told, "Don't be ridiculous! You're too young and female."

I thought if I did it once, I could do it again; I've got the business training, the brains, and the perseverance. My opportunity came almost immediately. There was to be a major convention in Seattle for hospital administrators, and since recruiting firms do most of their marketing at conventions it was critical that I attend. (There are always a couple of thousand people at the medical conventions — exhibitors, physicians, hospital administrators, and recruiting firms. Once you're in the convention scene, people start knowing you.) I literally had to incorporate, get cards printed, make travel arrangements — everything — in 48 hours. The printer I used had been conned by my former company, and he said to me, "Cynthia, if I have to work day and night to get these cards out for you, I will" — and that's exactly what he did.

My former employers were at the Seattle convention, too, and before I arrived everyone who knew me asked them where I was, not knowing, of course, I was no longer with them. They told people I was busy somewhere else, and suddenly I appeared. When I handed my new business card to people, my former employers tried to throw me out of the hotel, but of course they couldn't do that since I was legitimately registered. A lot of people were really enthusiastic about what I was doing, and when I threw a cocktail party (a standard procedure of recruiting firms), everyone showed up, even though my former employers discouraged them from attending. My party was so crowded, people were outside in the hallway. It was really very encouraging.

Soon after the Seattle convention, some hospital administrators, with whom I had previously placed physicians, gave me contracts, and within three weeks, I closed out these contracts, which is almost unheard of. One of the administrators told me, "Everybody's watching you. The one thing about you, no matter what you've done, you've always been a professional, and as young as you are,

while my former company would have gotten the money for having sent him up. Here I was trying to be on the administrator's side by being honest with him and he had crossed me up. The board has now come back to me and said, "We think you should be compensated for the time you spent with him." I was really pleased, but I didn't accept payment since that was not our original agreement.

I always believe I can find a person. It's just a matter of time. It's harder to get the contract, again, because of the reasons I've already mentioned about being a woman in business and being so young. Beyond that, people are reluctant to award me a contract because there's not a large organization behind me. They say, "What can one person do? What's your capacity?" I'm always up against that. That's a problem. My track record is very good, and I have to keep plugging away, and the more I keep getting contracts and closing them, the more I can say, "Hey look! I've closed so many searches in your state." What's more, my searches have always been so impossible. I've been forced into taking on the types of searches no one else has been able to solve, but by perseverance I have succeeded.

For instance, one hospital had difficulty recruiting a pediatrician. The hospital was nice, the area was nice. I thought, "What's the problem here?" I started doing some investigating, asking a lot of questions, cross-referencing with people, and really getting them to open up. Then I found that the head pediatrician would run off any candidate because he felt threatened by any physician who might come in. He thought it would hurt his practice. I thought, okay, now I know what I have to do. I'm going to go and talk to this doctor, but talk to him in a way where he's not threatened by me and he won't think, "Who's this person telling me what to do?" I didn't want to tell him anything. I wanted him to reach his own conclusions, so I started asking him a lot of questions.

"What would happen if another physician came into town?"

"Oh," he said, "my practice would decrease," and he proceeded to list all the possible problems.

I asked him, "How much vacation time have you taken in the last year?"

"None."

"What do you like to do in your spare time?"

"I'd do anything if I could travel," he said, "but I just don't have the time."

So I suggested, "Maybe if you had someone else to help you out, you might get some time, and I don't think it would ruin your practice. If anything, it may help."

I started explaining why and went into detail about it, and after that I had no trouble getting someone in there. It had been necessary to change his thinking and make him understand that another pediatrician wouldn't cut into his practice and, in the end, he was very pleased.

The recruiting field requires a lot of dedication and perseverance. It's a lot of work. It's not unusual for me to work an 18-to-20 hour day. When things are going well, it's just super. I'm on cloud nine. The successful closing of a contract can amount to a lot of money for me. However, unless the contracts are coming in consistently, you're always going through a cash-flow problem. You have to learn how to budget in order to provide for the dry months.

My life has always been like a roller coaster. It's either feast or famine. The dry spells can be very, very frustrating and extremely depressing, because as the owner of my own company, I'm out there all by myself. Sometimes I say, "Oh, God, why did I do this?" I think there's something inside of me that just says, "Well, what if Columbus had given up, or what if Edison hadn't persevered the fiftieth time?"

My struggle has provided a source of conflict with my family. We're extremely close, but since I've started my own company, my mother has been urging me at 25 years of age to work for a nice, solid, secure firm and receive a steady pay check. My father was a salesman, and he understands that sometimes you're knocking on doors and nothing happens, while another time you're going to go in and someone's going to give you the account.

My parents are a product of the depression and the wars when economic security was essential. I'm not saying it isn't important. I'd like to know I don't have to worry about money, but at the same time, this company means everything to me. Do you realize what it means to me when I get a call after other established organizations have bid on a contract and I'm one they've selected? Me? One person, Cynthia Paulis? To win that contract? That's a big step. People are recognizing that my reputation is good—that my work is good. "Mom," I say, "Even Mobil Oil started out as a small company."

We come through on this earth just once. We take things and we put things back. I want to put something back. When I do a good job, other people are going to benefit. That is really important to me. I always feel after being awarded a contract and I get on the search for people, "Oh, good. Whom will I be playing Santa Claus for today?"

There are a lot of other things I still want to do. It really frustrates me to feel I have only one life. How much can I cram into one life? Maybe I want to play doctor, lawyer, Indian chief, or do them all. Most people think I'm really crazy. They say, "You should do only one thing and just work at that." I don't agree. I feel you should try to do a variety of things, and in that way you really learn about who you are as a person and what you're the best at.

When I walk away from a community — such as a rural community where they've needed a physician for so long — I get a tremendous amount of satisfaction and pride after seeing the facial expressions of the physician, the spouse, the administrator, and the hospital directors, and, most important, the community members. Everyone's happy, and I think, "Wow! I've really affected a positive change there."

A year and a half later, Cynthia told us she had applied to medical school and was accepted.

I will be closing down my company in August 1980 and moving on to a new set of goals and achievements. After being involved with rural communities, I hope to return to one of those towns and open a practice in family medicine. After I graduate in four years, with my business, health care, and medical background, I'll have more options open. Who knows, I may still get to play doctor, lawyer, and Indian chief.

Naomi Fisher

DESIGNER, MANUFACTURER, AND RETAILER OF QUILTS,
Bird in Hand, Lancaster County, Pennsylvania.

*Guilt sometimes provided the motivation to start a business. Women
who were used to generating their own income often felt guilty when
they stopped contributing an income to raise their children.*

I felt guilty spending my husband's money that he made at the
trailer factory. It was also my money, but then again, I needed things
and I felt guilty just using it however I wanted to, without trying to
help. When Mary Sue, our youngest one, was about a year and a half
old, I started the quilts.

My husband and I were rather old when we got married. I was 24 and
he was 27, so we both thought we had a lot of money saved up.
Before we moved into this house, we remodeled the whole thing and
we spent around $20,000. Right away, where was the money? I had
to do something to help along, so I made homemade bread for a couple of years and sold it along the road here, but it was so much work
and I had to do it even when the weather was hot. I really got tired of
making bread. After the third child came along, I didn't do anything
extra for a year. Then I felt that I just had to do something. So I started
the quilts.

I made one quilt and decided to sell it, but I thought I might as well sell a couple more at the same time, so I bought a few and sold them. Now women make quilts, bring them here, and I sell them on consignment. People that I have never even known before come in with a couple of quilts in their arms and say, "Would you like to sell this for me?" I don't have the heart to refuse them. There are some that are not as good quality. I just don't mark them up as high, and I tell the women that I'll try to do the best I can with their quilts. Some people are very much in a hurry — "I've got to get this done and get it out and get my money." Others will do quilting that is very fine and are very careful with their stitches. There is also a difference in quality of material. Most people use 65% Dacron and 35% cotton, a very nice blend that's washable and doesn't have to be ironed. I charge by the amount and quality of the work, the kinds of materials used, and how well the colors coordinate. I can tell what a quilt is worth right away.

My business is seasonal, but I'm busy all the time because in winter I'm busy with women coming in wanting work. I design many quilts, and there's around five people piecing quilts for me most all the time. First the whole top must be sewed together. If you're making a log cabin design, you have to make 16 pieces of each patch, and you have to make 80 patches, ten patches long and eight patches wide. It takes around eight yards for the top and eight yards for the back. For piecing, we have a flat rate. We usually go by the size of the quilt and the number of patches. Most times we pay a woman around $35 or $40. I have one who is doing a log cabin, and she can do one in three days. She's really swift. After the patches are sewed together, and the border put on, I draw the quilting design on with a stencil. Then I get everything ready for the quilter.

We stretch the backing out in a big frame, put a whole layer of quilt padding in the center, put the top on, and stitch all three layers together. That's where the fancy quilt designs come in.

Twelve women, sometimes fifteen, quilt for me, depending on how busy the season is. In the winter, people can quilt much faster because they have more time. I pay the quilters by the yards of thread they use. I give them two spools of quilting thread, 250 yards on a spool, and they use anywhere from 250 yards to 450 yards per quilt.

I have many older women helping me because most times they're retired, their husbands have quit farming, and they're glad to make a little extra money. They're really not paid adequately for their time. If I charged the amount of money that their handiwork is worth, I'd be pricing myself right out of the market.

The most fun is designing the quilt. I really enjoy that. Of course, I enjoy selling them, too. It's really a pleasure when you're able to sell a quilt to someone who loves it.

The location of my home makes a big difference. We're not along the main track, but we're not as far off as some people are. People in the back woods couldn't do what I'm doing. They bring their quilts here to sell because they don't feel they could sell them where they live. There are many gift shops around that would like to buy my quilts and resell them, and sometimes they do, too, but they find that the prices are pretty high for them to put on another $50 or $100. A lot of people who come here have been sent by other places in the community that sell things and display our little cards. Our card has a map on the back so that they can find us. I don't have a telephone, so my husband took some cards here and there one day last winter. Just last week, a woman from the Pennsylvania Dutch Tourist Bureau came in and asked for cards. She said she has people coming in asking for quilts, and she'd like to know where to send them. She thought my collection was one of the best she has seen.

The first year, we sent out black-and-white brochures. The next year, we sent the same brochure, but we added a colored photograph and a couple of samples of material. When I stuffed the envelope with the brochure and the pictures and samples, I'd write on the brochure, would they please return the picture or send 75¢. Most people would do either one or the other and said they'd like this or that quilt and order one. Others would send the money or just do nothing, but what I like about it best was that I got an answer one way or the other, and I kind of got a feel from the people of what they were thinking, if they like them and were sometime going to order.

The quilt business has really helped us a lot. The main thing is trying to get our debts paid off. We're concerned about the mortgage on the house. Now I don't feel as guilty as I did when I wasn't helping out. I tell myself, "You're making some money. You can afford it." If I need something, I'll buy it.

For information write: Naomi Fisher, 2807 Church Road, Bird in Hand, Pennsylvania 17505.

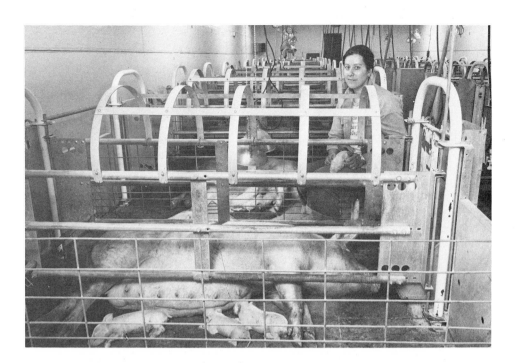

Kathleen Barbier

PORK PRODUCER,
Yorkville, Illinois.

Some women open businesses that relate back to experiences that they had when they were young. Katie Barbier had a pet pig when she was growing up. Professional animal breeding requires carefully controlled care since breeding animals for food purposes is essentially a numbers game — the maximum number of live births consistently produced from the maximum number of litters from each bred female. It's a high-risk business, given fluctuating costs of feed and medical care along with fluctuating prices. After controlling variables — such as sickness, which erodes profits — Katie feels that breeding pigs for food can enable a woman to earn a good living for herself.

My parents farmed when I was a little girl, and one day the sow house fell on the sow. They brought a surviving baby pig into the house and put her in the oven to keep her warm. She became very affectionate and as she grew up, she became our watch dog. The landlord was afraid of that pig because it would bark and defend the gate, and he wouldn't step foot on our property.

A few years ago, I had another pet pig that I got down at the Joliet stockyards. A sow had farrowed, and my 4-H kids and I brought home nine baby pigs. Of the nine, mine was the only one that lived. I worked for a vet at the time and I took the pig to work every day in a little dog crate in my Porsche. Every time he'd get up, I'd cram a Playtex nurser into his mouth. If I'd walk out of the room, he'd scream. I was his mother, and he'd follow me everywhere. I started weaning him when he got to about 30 pounds. I thought, "I can't be bottle feeding him the rest of his life." I would put water in the bottle, but he knew the difference between the milk and the water. I'd put him out in a pen, and I could walk out there, not say a word, and he'd start screaming. He knew by the smell that I was there and I was going to feed him. I said, "Sorry, Pinky, but you're either going to eat or starve." One day I mixed dog food for the dogs and then fed them all at the same time. Pinky needed an influence to look down and eat. From that time on, he ate dog food. If you threw a stick, he'd chase it and bring it back. He'd chase cars, or jump over the log pile and, with our two dogs, run to a neighbor's to play with their dog. I thought then, "Some day I'd really love to raise baby pigs."

When my parents bought this farm, my brother brought me a set of bred gilts. (Bred gilts are virgin pigs that are going to "pig" or farrow for the first time. After they "pig" their first litter, they're considered a sow.) I cleaned out a chicken coop and put a few crates in there, and that's how I started farrowing. Now it takes Dave, my teenage assistant, and me two days to clean the farrowing house just as white as we can get it. Everybody says I'm noted for the cleanest farrowing house in the county. It's probably helped cut down diseases.

The drudgery is worth it, for the best part of it all is having the babies. It's amazing to see the little pigs come out with teeth, fighting. They're the toughest little things. Within three days they're just fat, plump, gorgeous little pigs. Their bodies just seem to swell up after they get their iron shot.

It's not a 9-to-5 job. I was up till 3:30 this morning farrowing some litters. It happens only six times a year for one week. Then it's all day long or all night long until they're all farrowed. It takes one sow an average of two-and-a-half to three hours from farrow to finish.

When the pigs come out, we pick them up and cut the cord the length of their feet. We dry them off and clean their noses out right away. I make sure the sow doesn't lie on them or that the little pigs don't get caught in the cracks behind the sow where the manure falls through or that they don't wind up on the cold cement. You have it 80 degrees in there and the cement is still too cold. They come out of 102 degrees into an 80-degree atmosphere, and they shake. I stick them in a box under the heat lamp. Even so, there's no way they're all going to be taken care of.

A lot of farmers around here think I'm nuts for sitting up all night long. I don't know whether I've saved more that way. Probably I have. Those born wrapped up in the afterbirth can't breathe. They've become big healthy pigs, but if they were left there, they'd have suffocated. I can also check the sow and see that her bags are milking okay. If not, I give her a shot to relax her so the milk can flow and the babies can nurse. When the sow is ready to feed her babies, she grunts, which starts the milk flowing. The milk flows for one minute only, which is why there is such a scramble for the teats. When the sow stops grunting, the milk stops flowing until the next feeding time.

I lot-breed my sows rather than use artificial insemination. I have four boars, which is more than enough boar power. If a boar is fully mature and developed, like the ones I have now, he can handle five or six sows in a day. Two of them work the same sow, and then I rotate them, two for day, two for night, so I've got four boars for the same pen. One will stand and wait until the other one gets through. One is always more aggressive.

Pigs hold their domain. I have three pens for my sows, and if I put a sow in a pen she has not been in before, a couple of the girls will come up and start picking on her. "She's new. She doesn't belong here. She doesn't smell right." And they'll nail her. The boars don't like fights, and they'll take care of any problems. The sows respect the boars.

A sow's diet while gestating is four pounds a day. When they go into the farrowing house, it's seven pounds a day. After they farrow, it's ten to twelve pounds. A boar's diet is five pounds a day. You get a fat sow or a fat boar and they don't work, so you try to keep them a good weight.

You can get two-and-a-half litters out of a sow a year. I'm getting two litters. The other part of the year, the sows are in the process of being bred or gestating, which takes three months, three weeks, and three days. That's where the half comes from. You breed them so that they will farrow when they are a year old. You can breed them at six months, but the more heats they have, the more pigs they'll give birth to and the better average you're going to have on your gilts.

When I first started in 1977, my average was four out of 30 gilts. That means an average of four pigs survived out of each litter and I had sows that did not farrow at all. This year I have finally hit about an eight. In my last farrowing, I had eight-to-nine, and I'm hoping that by the first of next year, the business will begin to start paying. You've got to have a better-than-eight average to make money.

Disease is a major problem in the hog business. SMEDI, for instance, is a disease common to hogs which causes stillborns, mummification, and embryonic death to the fetuses of gilts and sows. A hog that has SMEDI after 30 days of pregnancy may abort or the fetus may die. When the pig delivers that fetus, it looks like a mummy. If the pig has SMEDI in the last term of pregnancy, she will give birth to stillborns. When a pig has SMEDI, from one tube she may deliver a good pig, two mummies, a stillborn, and two good ones, and from the other tube she may deliver three good ones, a mummy, and a still. This is the problem I had when I had my four average. Three farrowings were affected by this disease.

I have about 500 pigs. My farrowing goal is 1,500 a year. My costs are feed, veterinary, trucking, electricity, etc. Roughly, if I sell 1,200 hogs, I should gross between $100,000 to $120,000 a year. Taking out expenses, I will probably net $40,000, but this has not quite been achieved.

My commercial herd includes hogs to sell as feeder pigs or to keep myself and raise until I sell them at Joliet stockyards to Swift or Armour or whoever wants to give me the best buck. Feeder pigs are little ones that weigh 40 pounds. A buyer who buys 40-pound feeder pigs is eliminating all the worry and the headaches of getting the pigs from birth to 40 pounds. After 40 pounds, you just put feed in the feeders and make sure the water is clean. The pigs are marketable for meat at 220 pounds. I'm running about five-and-a-half months to get them to that weight. During the winter, it takes six months or more.

A butcher is a 220-pound pig. You'll never get a 25-pound ham from it because 40% is bone or waste. Big picnic hams that are 25 pounds at the supermarket are from a sow, not from a butcher. One sow that I sold weighed 450 pounds. I paid top dollar for her when I bought her. She put out maybe four or five litters, and she'd paid for herself by the time I sold her.

When a male goes to market he is a barrow — a castrated boar. Boars give off body smells. You don't want to castrate them when they're 200 pounds, so I make that determination at three weeks old. Some of them I make at two months if they've got ruptures or they're real runts. My vet showed me how to castrate them.

I have a gooseneck fifth-wheel trailer, and I can ship 32 hogs at a crack. It takes about an hour to load if everything goes all right and they're cooperative and don't run under the trailer or jump all over. I take them myself to the Joliet stockyards. I back up the trailer, unload them, and they're run down an alleyway and are put in a pen with feeders and automatic water troughs.

When I first went down with the feeder pigs four years ago, I was the only woman who did this. The guys about dropped their teeth. They couldn't believe it. They said, "My God! Look at the woman backing the truck up!" They'd fall over themselves to help unload it After a while, they just figured, "Oh, here comes Katie. She can do it on her own." My commission man told me, "We enjoy having you come down. You add a little sunshine to everything."

My commission man is very proud of me. He goes to the representative for Armour and says, "O.K., I've got 33 hogs. They're Katie's." He just has to say Katie and, "Oh yeah? Let's go look at them." They've seen my hogs cut out. They've followed them to the packer. They know what my loin is, and how my bacon looks, and how much back fat I've got, and they know that my hog is a fairly decent hog. They're going to pay top dollar for it. When I first started going down there, I never missed topping the market for that day. One of the neighbors used to call up and ask, "Is Katie going to be there today? I'm not shipping if Katie's going to be there. She takes a quarter off of my family's table."

I don't get much for pigs with real ugly ruptures or for pigs that are arthritic or skuzzy —10¢ or a quarter a pound, but it's better than having them die. I take them down to Joliet. The man who buys them is a butcher, and he makes sausage meat out of them for pizzas. It's a big joke because I say, "Well, I sold a couple of my hogs for pizzas."

My brother and I went from a very small business into what is now going to be a very big business. I do the labor. He's good at the bank.

I'm not that business minded—I never had the opportunity to do it—but within the last six months, I've learned a lot. I'm becoming more of a businesswoman than I ever thought I'd be. I never thought I had enough brains in my head.

I'm now considering a new building. It would have a mill in the end of it so that I wouldn't have to hand grind. Now I have a grinder that I hook up to a tractor, and I lift 50-pound bags of protein, which is bean meal and alfalfa meal, and I mix my own premix calibrating vitamins and calcium. I dump that all in the grinder, fill it up with corn, and then auger it into the feeders. By putting in a mill, I would push a few buttons and the augers would bring it down, and I wouldn't have to do a lot of bending and backwork.

Another advantage of the new building would be to protect the pigs from the elements. The lots that my pigs sit in now are outside lots, and the feeders are outside, which means handling a lot of manure and also means there are deaths due to cold weather. I lost a pig-and-a-half a day outside during the month of January 1979 during our big blizzard. They pile up on top of each other and they get prolapses, which are like hemorrhoids in the rectum. A prolapse will heal, but the rectum hole closes and they can't pass gas and they blow up and die. The new house will protect them from the cold and will be slatted for the manure to fall through, and there's very little labor in it.

I don't know where I want to be in five years. I haven't thought about it, probably because I've had so many sicknesses with the hogs and so many problems. I want a ten-point average. I want fat, happy, big pigs. You have to have super genetic lines and good milkers and long bodies with lots of teats that are all going to make milk. Eventually I'd like to have a restaurant, maybe, and sell my pork chops.

Susan Ziffrin Spak

ADVERTISING
CONSULTANT
AND SALES
REPRESENTATIVE,
Barrington, Illinois.

The women we interviewed who were company sales representatives were not given an office with a desk. Because they had to maintain their own offices from their homes, the Internal Revenue Service categorizes them as home business owners.

Is an office just a room or is an office a desk in the family room? We have to have a place to do our paperwork and record keeping. The company has an office with a secretary. The regional manager has a desk, there's a conference room, and that's it! I do my paperwork, take care of my phone calls, stamp individualized matchbooks, and prepare generally for prospective clients at home.

I wanted to be an actress. My mother and father said if I finished college and got a teaching degree, I'd always have that behind me, and if I still wanted to be an actress, I could go out and be an actress. So I got a teaching degree. In my last year of college, I got married. My husband was still in college, and I couldn't afford to be an actress, so I started teaching — and I taught for eleven years. After we moved out of the city, I had to drive an hour and a half to my job every day, and it got to be a bit much. By then, my husband was more financially secure.

There was a very small retail clothing store for sale three miles from my house and I bought it. Having set a goal of having X dollars in gross sales within a five-year period, I reached my goal exactly three years to the day. That same day I sold the business.

I started looking at want ads for work in sales, because I had enjoyed sales at the clothing store, and I became a salesperson of educational materials but that job ended quickly when school revenues were decreased and school systems no longer made great expenditures for textbooks.

Then, when I was working for a pinball machine manufacturer at the Chicago Advertising Age Convention, I met a vice-president of the Universal Match Company, who invited me to come and talk with his company. Just for a kick, I had an interview with the regional manager, and after a third meeting, the second vice-president said, "Susan, I think you'd be fine for us." I had given it a lot of thought. The money was relatively good to begin with and the earning possibilities seemed just endless, so I took the job.

For two weeks I sat in an office with a closed door and I learned about matches. They're very complicated. Quality in a matchbook means fine paper stock. It means that when you strike a match, sulfur won't fly all over and burn your clothes or go into your eye. Quality also means the striker. If you strike 20 or 28 matches from the same book, inferior strikers are virtually gone. The printing on quality matches is fine. The smallest type is still readable. Other considerations are paper stock, the number of colors, where you can print, and how much more it costs if you have a map on the inside of the matchbook.

Even if they give someone a match, people keep the book. Each matchbook is used 20, 28 times. A study of matchbooks thrown down on the sidewalk in one of the major cities showed that there were, at most, two matches left in a matchbook.

Matchbook advertising is rather subliminal. If you keep using matches that say "Tums for the tummy," you will be likely to buy Tums if you have an upset stomach. If you're a nonsmoker, you have candles, or a fireplace, or a barbecue, and you use matches. There are always matches in the home in case of an emergency or for guests. And people collect matches. If the match is just a beautiful product, if it's artistically and tastefully done, you'll comment on the match. There are just so many possibilities, so much you can do with and to a match that I had never thought about before.

Anyway, I took the job, and I succeeded in placing an order with the first person I went to, a friend who owns a restaurant. Well, I could not contain myself. I was absolutely ecstatic. That was the beginning.

My most difficult sale was one to my husband's commercial printing company. I went through a presentation on matchbook advertising with my brother-in-law Jay, who was responsible for advertising and marketing, but he said, "Susan, we don't want matches, we can't use matches, and we don't need matches." Behind me was Jay's son, who worked there, and I said quite frankly to Jay, "You're not supporting anyone in my family. You don't see my mother, my sister, my kids working here. All I'm asking you to do is to buy some matches. They'll be beneficial to you."

He said, "Susan, no," and then he came right out and asked, "What is your commission on this?" I blurted out $200. I hadn't figured it yet. "Fine," he said. "I'll write you a personal check for $200 if you'll just go away and leave us alone."

Well then my dander was up. "Absolutely not," I said. "It's not too much to ask. You're getting a minimum quantity of matches. Now it's more of a psychological thing with me that my family, my husband's family business, would not support a wife who's really out there trying to sell matches."

"Well," he said, "all right. I'll buy matches, but our big show is not for eight months. I'll sign the order now just so you will leave me alone and won't bother me for eight months." I said, "All right. Fine."

I designed a beautiful matchbook and after they saw it, they were so excited and so enthusiastic about having their *own* matches, they asked me to send a special memo into my company asking that production be hurried up so that they could get their matches much before their date.

Another extremely difficult sale was at a savings and loan where I dealt with the vice-president, who was a very tough woman. She said, "I'll buy them from you if you give me the best price." She was getting competitive bids. I came to her with the price *I'm* authorized to make and she called and said, "Susan, I understand your figures, but that's not good enough. Go back to your boss and see if you can give me a better offer."

When I went back to my boss and told him he'd have to give her a better price, he gave me a price *he's* authorized to give, but when I went back to this woman she said, "It's not good enough. I have a bid from a competitor that is less than the price you gave me, and he too has a quality item." For some reason or other, she and I respected each other. We just hit it off beautifully. So she called me and said, "Because you are you, I'm going to tell you what the lower bid was. See if you can beat it." In the end we came in with a lower price. The company asked me if I was willing to take a 1% commission instead of the usual 10%, 12%, or 16%, and I said yes, because it was just the idea that this woman had done something for me. I was very happy with that sale of 300,000 matchbooks, because our minimum sale is 50,000.

At our first sales meeting, all the men just sat there and didn't talk to me. I think they were thinking I was never going to make it, because it's tough selling matches. And then at the meeting the month after that, when they discovered that my sales figures, for only being with the company a month, were very good, they said hello to me. The next month, they talked to me a little bit more, although they were a little wary. I still have to prove that I can do it and see if they accept me.

We don't have business cards per se, we have a set of six matchbooks, and at that first sales meeting I put my matches on the table—my calling cards as it were. They said "Susan Z. Spak, Sales Representative." Those of the fellow on my right said "Jim blank, blank, Advertising Consultant," and those of the chap on my left said "Tim so-and-so, Advertising Consultant." When I asked my boss, "Why are they advertising consultants and I'm a sales representative?" he said, "When I ordered them, I was in a hurry." I didn't press the issue until about two weeks ago, when one of the other salesmen in the office called an account I had been working on since December, not knowing that I too had been working on it, and the important man in control returned the other salesman's call although he had not returned any of mine. I called this important man's secretary and said, "This is Susan at Universal Match Company. Why is it that Mr. so-and-so just called one of our salesmen?" "Because his calling card said 'Advertising Consultant,' " she said, "and we thought he might have been in a more important position than you." So the title really wasn't important until I saw how other people were viewing it. Since then, I've talked to the president of the company and

I'm having new matchbooks printed up that say "Advertising Consultant."

The harder I work, the more I sell. Sometimes the company furnishes us with leads. People from the company go to a number of shows like the Advertising Age Convention, and hand out a little questionnaire, "Would you be interested in hearing about matchbook advertising?" If the prospective client says yes, he fills in his name, address, and phone number and I'm given the lead card, and I call and make an appointment. So that is simple. The people already have expressed interest.

Often I drive down the street and stop in a restaurant and look at their matchbook. If it's not Universal's, I give them a bid. They might have a matchbook that's so cluttered, you can't read anything. Nothing is important because there's just so much on it. I suggest that they might want to change. Being an artist, I'm able to take an existing matchbook and design a matchbook cover right in front of them. I say, "Of course I'm just trying to give you an idea of how your matchbook is going to look. The art department will come back with a finished product."

I once went to a ski lodge and noticed that the name was written one way on the menu, in another type on the current matches, and in a third type style on the sign outside. I walked in and said, "Sir, don't you think we should coordinate all of these signs into one logo, one design for everything you have here?" It's a ski lodge, a summer recreational area, a tennis court complex, a disco, a restaurant, a lounge, and a motel, and condominiums are going to be built on the property. It was a total recreational environment. It was very unusual for me to do this, but I said, "Don't sign an order. Let me take all of these ideas and send them to our art department and see what they can come up with." I wrote up a two-page description of what his facility was going to be and I incorporated the idea of total recreational environment. The people in the art department came back with two designs which I showed to the owner of the complex, and he was so thrilled with our matchbook design, he is now using that type style and logo on everything he puts into his establishment.

On days when I haven't had appointments, I've gone out at 8:00 A.M. and made cold calls at cleaners, restaurants, and other places and gotten absolutely nowhere. When I do this 15 or 16 times in a day, I get a little down in the dumps, so I stop. I go home and try to get appointments so I know that the next day I have an important call first thing in the morning, or maybe last thing in the afternoon in case I have another bad day. If

I have an important call at 3:00 P.M., then I'm ready for it. I much prefer working by appointment because then people know I'm from Universal Match Company and am there to sell matchbook advertising, so psychologically we've gotten over that barrier. Prior to an appointment, I put the prospective client's name into my Franklin Hot Stamping Machine and I stamp out ten matchbooks for him. It's just a little extra thank you for allowing me to see him with or without the sale.

My schedule is dictated by my 6- and 8-year-old daughters, because that's the way I want it. I put them on the school bus at 7:55 A.M. and go directly to work. I don't stop for lunch, but I'm at the school bus at 3:30 to pick them up. Then I call the office to get my messages, because fortunately people do call me every day. The first time I called in at 3:30, my boss asked why I was home so early and I said, "My hours are from 8:00 to 3:30." "Susan," he said, "we expect you to work until five o'clock." And I told him that in our first interview, I had made it quite clear that my children come first. "When I'm working, I work hard and I devote myself to my job, but the children come first."

Last week one of my children was sick, and I wasn't going to leave her, so I called the office and said to my boss, "I know you don't understand, because you are a man and you have no children, but I have a sick child and I'm not going to work today." He said, "Susan, you have to do what you think is right." Of course, I have guilt feelings. I'm being paid to work, but then, if I had left my child, those guilt feelings would have been greater, and no job is worth that, even if I do like the job and I'm good at it.

There was a period of two months in my life when I didn't work. I developed a ringing in my ears. I was very irritable with my children and my husband because I did nothing all day. I didn't care if I got dressed. I'd get up and eat breakfast with the children, and I'd eat lunch with them. As soon as lunch was over, I'd begin thinking about what we were going to have for dinner. I cleaned the house all day, which I don't mind doing, but it was really very dull. My husband would come home from work and ask, "What did you do today?" "Nothing." It was not healthy for my children, my husband, or myself. I have to work for my own well being.

A few months after our interview, Susan told us she asked her boss for a leave of absence until the children were back in school for the fall session. Her boss consented.

Jonna Castle

INDEPENDENT CONTRACTOR FOR LUNCHEON IS SERVED,
Denver, Colorado.

Even though 12 of the women we interviewed had aligned them-selves with already existing companies or organizations, all of them worked from or maintained necessary offices in their own homes:

> *Two of them manufactured company-designed clothes as independent contract workers.*

> *Two performed primarily secretarial functions for a company.*

> *Four sold a company's products or services on a commission basis as employees of the company.*

> *Four were independent contractors whose guidelines and major policies were set by the company.*

Luncheon Is Served, a national company with independent contrac-tors in 50 cities throughout the United States, promotes products of other companies by sponsoring fund-raising buffets for nonprofit groups. Like Avon, Amway, Shaklee, Tupperware, and others, it bases its marketing and distribution techniques on individuals who maintain home offices and home warehousing.

Every woman is more or less an independent businesswoman

who works for the company. Many of us go to a central warehouse because the products have to be stored in bulk, but most of the women work just as I do, right out of their own homes. My company pays me a small fee for storage because I use my garage as a warehouse.

Three years ago, when I was looking in the newspapers for a job, I saw an ad that called for an unusual housewife. Although I didn't really consider myself an unusual housewife, the ad went on to say that it was a part-time job and you would be your own boss, and I was interested for those reasons.

The lady who had placed the ad flew from California to Denver to interview me. She let me know the next day that I was hired. Then she gave me a three-hour briefing on how to run this business and she went back to California and left me with it.

I hadn't worked for a number of years. I had done a lot of volunteer work and a lot of part-time secretarial work, but I hadn't worked in a really responsible position. It wasn't long before I began to realize just how responsible it was and the tremendous load that I was going to have to carry. The season opened in September with two bookings on the same day, a luncheon for 125 people and a dinner for 200. I just simply called up the lady from California and said, "Look, you're going to have to come back and help me," and so she did.

The purpose of the luncheon we serve is to raise funds for nonprofit groups. While we charge them a small service fee, our income comes from various major food companies that pay us to advertise their products. They supply all the products and pay all the shipping costs.

We try to reach as many different people as we can. For that reason, we work with each club only once each year. In a 10-month period we do between 160 and 200 luncheons and dinners — or from four to ten a week.

Very often a company that is introducing a product into this area uses our services as a means of introduction. For instance, we advertised for a good number of months for Armour Chili, which you couldn't buy in Denver. They wanted to create sufficient demand so that the supermarkets would stock it. A lot of companies use us for this reason.

We also do research and testing of new products. A small local company here is always coming up with something new, and very often they call us to test it and get a consumer opinion. J. R. Kennedy Company just came out with a product that we promoted for a couple of months at our luncheons, but we also tested it for Mr. Kennedy before he put it on the market to see what the public reaction would be. Coffee Stretch costs 69¢ and comes in a little envelope that you mix with a pound of coffee to make your coffee go twice as far. Mr. Kennedy wanted to see if people would notice a difference in the taste — and they did not. The public reaction was very acceptable, so he decided to put it on the market. We've done testing for other manufacturers, too, and saved them quite a bit of money. We've also had instances when a product didn't go over well, and the companies decided that either it needed improvements or maybe it just wasn't a good thing to go ahead and market.

Each company pays us so much per luncheon for advertising its product. Those fees vary according to what we do for them and how many products are involved. There's a flat basic fee, but it varies according to a number of factors. Some companies may wish to promote, say, in Chicago, Denver, and San Francisco, and then, of course, their fees would probably be somewhat lower per promotion than if they were just doing it in Denver.

The products change. Some companies stay with us for a number of years, and others are with us for perhaps a season. A contract runs anywhere from six months to a whole season of ten months. I had 21 sponsors this year.

We serve buffet style, so the people serve themselves. Some companies want their product served plain so that people can get the real taste of it. Others encourage us to do things to make it prettier, fancier, and tastier.

After the meal is completed, I give a presentation on the various products and I give away gifts from the companies. Just about every company provides free or discount coupons. The ladies almost need a shopping bag to take home the goodies that we provide them. Some items are not available in every supermarket, and I let the women know where they can be purchased.

I try to keep the presentation to 20 minutes, but that isn't easy to do, since some companies have more than one product for us to use or promote. For instance, although we serve only one item for Golden Grain Company, we promote about 15 of its products. We don't want a hard sell. The basic advertising, of course, is in the tasting itself. We try to give each company up to a minute and a half. Most often we are the sole presentation, but some organizations add a fashion show or card party or some entertainment.

We have a busy season and a slack season. We go great guns in spring, because that is when groups want to have luncheons and style shows and so forth. The slack season is in December and January, when the clubs are having their Christmas parties.

The nonprofit organizations determine the place where we will work. We just ask that they have adequate kitchen and dining facilities. We do a lot of church groups and Masonic groups which do have such facilities.

We have arrived to fix a luncheon and found no stove and no sink. One time, for example, we served in a new church that didn't yet have a kitchen. There was no refrigerator, no sink, except for a little hand-washing sink down the hall, no work space, and no counters. There was an apartment-size stove with only two burners, and the oven was not big enough for our pans, so we simply found some women who lived close enough to the church and made use of their stoves. The church had children's Sunday School tables that came up to our knees, so we just made the best of it — we got down on our knees and laughed all the way through the preparation and serving of a meal for 125 people.

We charge the companies one fee for the first 125 people, and this season the fee has been $55 for the evening and $45 for the lunch. I kick back $10 to Luncheon Is Served, which helps to cover some of the bookkeeping that they do for me. The rest of it is mine, so in one evening I make $45 for three and a half hours of work.

Some items are not delivered to me, and I don't get paid for picking up them up. I have to do all the paperwork, keep up the inventory and cope with all the problems. If I really wanted to break it down into really fine print, I don't make quite $10 an hour, but I find that I've been able to organize myself well enough so that I really can keep the time to a minimum.

I'd like to be more involved in recruiting companies to use our service for their advertising. Luncheon Is Served does have a sales force that is basically responsible for making initial contacts and getting the contracts, and then it's up to me to maintain public relations. I get together with the vice-president or sales manager or the broker and go over what they want me to say and do for them, because each company has a different objective.

I hire people to work with me, and now I have an associate who does the same thing I do, so when we have two presentations on the same day, it's no problem because she does one and I do one. Another woman does phoning for me to line us up with clubs and organizations, and she also makes out the schedule for me. I don't know two months in advance, without asking her, if I have something scheduled for a certain day, but she keeps a schedule and sends a copy to me — and I take it from there. The women who work for me are really good. Although the company authorizes me to hire a third person for cooking, my women decided that they would rather work a little harder and take the extra money. I make out the schedule each month and present it to them so they know when they're supposed to work, and if there's a day that they don't want to work, they simply contact one of the other women and let me know of the change. They have been supercooperative about making sure that nobody's short-handed, and they work it out among themselves.

I just can't begin to give enough credit to them. There is such a good spirit. I don't think that the job itself is that much fun. What's fun about going into a hot kitchen and fixing a meal in an hour and a half for 125 people over and over? The fun of it is they all know and like each other, and it gives them a chance to gossip and talk.

There are some problems with this business. By having it in my home, I'm completely surrounded by it all the time. The job never stops. It's not as though I can leave the office and go home and forget it. The telephone rings constantly, and sometimes it seems like I have a telephone attached to my ear.

I also have had some real hassles with the trucking companies who deliver products. They're union men and they have regulations, so some of them just set the products in the middle of the street, and I've had to carry them in. They often want to charge me an additional fee for residential delivery, but I've managed to avoid paying that. Most of them, however, have been really very nice and very, very generous.

Sometimes I've been very nervous about the big semitrailers that pull up in front of my house and unload things. I've just simply kept my fingers crossed and depended on the good will and good nature of my neighbors not to complain. When we have leftover food from our luncheons, I share it with my neighbors.

About the advantages, however, I could go on and on. I don't have to get up and go out to an office every morning. If there's paperwork or telephoning to be done, I don't have to dress, because nobody's going to see me. I can have lunch or coffee any time. If I want to go out of town for a few days, I can arrange ahead of time not to schedule any luncheons for that day or simply have an associate do them if they're already scheduled. What I like most, however, is that Luncheon Is Served is a tremendous organization.

Sara Drower

DESIGNER AND CRAFTSWOMAN: SOFT SCULPTURE,
WALL HANGINGS, AND ONE-OF-A-KIND CLOTHING,
Wilmette, Illinois.

*The continuing isolation of women in their homes as they raise their
children may well be an impetus for the steadily growing number of
home craft businesses today. Over half of the craftswomen we interviewed developed their businesses after they had children. Having
talent, energy, and the need to care for their children motivates
women to draw on their own resources and create their own products. Home craft businesses are a natural solution for women in other
countries as well, for women engage in them throughout the world.*

When I visited China last year, I saw many people who worked in
little shops that were also their homes. The lady was in front sewing,
the cot was in the back, and her little stove was cooking away. There
are two kinds of crafts in China: production crafts for the export
market, which is human work reproducing what machines don't do,
and one-of-a kind pieces.

In Australia, there are a number of needlework and handworkers
societies. Women are highly organized in the domestic arts because
many of them live out in the country on remote stations or ranches.
They have many hours, if not weeks, without any kind of companion-

ship. The women keep their neat little homes and embroider and quilt and weave and spin yarn. They're not amateurs. They're very proficient. They have organized on a state and national level to show their work and to exchange with each other.

I was originally a biology teacher, although I had studied at the Art Institute of Chicago. I earned a lot of money free-lancing scientific illustrations.

After my first child was born, I tried teaching for one year, and it was really a hassle. The babysitter wouldn't show up the day I really had to be at the school. For about six months, I enjoyed staying home, cooking gourmet recipes, and taking care of my kid — and then the novelty wore off. By the time the second one came along, I had tried teaching and doing some free-lance jobs. Nothing was clicking. There were too many demands that little children impose.

My husband said, "You need a new interest and you need one night out a week." I wanted to take weaving at the Evanston Art Center, but weaving was filled, so I took a printmaking class.

It was a new medium to me. The talent that I'd always had, came back. It was refreshing to do something spontaneous instead of the rigors of scientific illustration where you have to stick to the subject matter. You can't add extra wings, and you can't add extra legs. A fellow in the class said, "Your stuff is really good. You ought to try to get into an art fair," and he gave me the name of a woman who ran art fairs for shopping centers. I didn't know what a top lady she was — she was very tough, like a sergeant in the army. I simply walked in with a portfolio of my little amateur prints from about six months in class, I dropped this guy's name, said he had sent me, and I'd like to be in her art fair. I found out later that he didn't even know her. It was just the chutzpah of the whole thing. I was using his name under false pretenses. Naiveté is sometimes your best protection.

Anyway, before I knew it, I was in her art fair. I had to start at the bottom and do the shabby fairs before she'd put me in the good ones, and I was always surprised when I sold something. I found myself in a show, and the rules said, "Paintings, drawings, sculpture. No prints," and they were emphatic about it. I had lithographs and etchings, which are clearly prints. I even called the lady up and she said, "Prints aren't art." Tell that to Picasso. Tell that to Rembrandt. Well, very quickly I needed a few drawings in order to justify all these prints that I would have. I had about five days to get my act together, and I figured if I did a drawing a day, I could just about get a nice little display together. I got my five pictures done and I won the second prize.

Now all of these things had a biological flavor. They were fine line and they were very intricate, a lot of leafy abstract shapes—all the things I really wanted to do. At that point, there was no stopping me. I made a whole bunch more of these drawings, and people bought them. I was working monochromatically, and the man who induced me to get into art fairs looked at me and he said, "Color sells. If you have a little bit of color, you'll sell more that if they're black and white." And so I added a little bit of color and he was right. And damn if I didn't get into a national drawing exhibit! Well suddenly I had a résumé, I had a couple of prizes, I had a couple of national shows, I enjoyed my art classes and the people that I hung around with. My work was starting to overwhelm our kitchen table and the family room and the dining room table.

The work became three-dimensional. My drawings had layers to them. They looked like dissected flat biology drawings. The only way to give myself depth was to do it in layers. After I'd visually done layers, I began to physically make layers. And physically the layers began to undulate. I formed paper that was wet, and when it would dry and harden I would draw on it. The pieces were starting to develop, but they'd only go so far. It was at a stage when the people were making a lot of handmade paper and doing three- dimensional things with paper and drawings.

Now anything that's three-dimensional is considered sculpture, but these were drawings, and so I straddled the line. I entered one as a drawing and one as a piece of sculpture in a drawing and sculpture ex- hibit. One got accepted as sculpture. Art was starting to break an awful lot of boundaries and barriers, and I enjoyed breaking them. If drawing occupied more than two dimensions, it enriched the mind. It took you to another level, yet it wasn't sculpture enough to call it sculpture. If a judge had this same sort of mental process, I would be accepted. It wasn't acclaimed, but it would be accepted. The terrible part about art is you're either accepted or rejected. The word rejected doesn't mean you're bad, it doesn't mean you're not good, it means it doesn't fit this exhibit. It's a very hard concept to accept because you're either in or out.

When things were not going as well for me and the work wouldn't get into a show, it would hurt deeply. After all, I had just gotten into a very good show, why didn't I get into all shows? I didn't have this easygoing feeling that I have now — that you can't win them all. You can't be *loved* by everybody. There were very conservative people who weren't willing to take a chance on it. The more you take a chance in doing something outlandish, the more you also have to suffer greater criticism and greater risk. I wasn't a good sport about it.

There were a number of reasons why I started doing work on fabric. One was that in my husband's business of selling plastics, he needed to prepare some iron-on fabric samples for a customer. The samples had to survive washing machines and the dry cleaners. At first my drawings on the samples came off in one or the other. I just love a challenge, and every time my drawings came off, I was more determined to find a permanent way to draw on cloth. When I would make a mistake, I would stuff all the pieces into a flower pot. I had seen the guy who made the little soft-sculpture cactus, and before you knew it, *I* had a whole little garden of cactus. I took them along to an art fair and sold them all. These little cactuses caught on. At the same time, art fairs were changing. Art purchases had dropped off. That's a real luxury item. Crafts were starting to rise. A craft is a utilitarian thing. There are crafts that are decorative and nonuseful, but crafts by and large are ceramics, glass, jewelry, something that has a purpose.

When I would do a piece of work on paper, it was considered a drawing. If I did the same thing on cloth, it was craft. If I did it on canvas, you'd call it a painting. If I left it hanging loose, it would be a wall hanging, and if I put it on a shirt, it's a craft. What's the difference? It's all the same art. The same talent went into the drawing. Oh, boy! Did it bother people.

I made a drawing and then sewed it up into a kid's dress. It was a drawing but the minute it could be worn, it was called a craft. Well, I had to rejury in my art fairs. I was in the wrong category. I was voted the best in show of crafts, and then they looked up and saw that I was registered in art. I didn't get my prize.

It happened at another show. A lady said to me, "Those aren't drawings." I said, "That clothing drawing has just been in a national drawing show. Why, the juror complimented it because it broke all the previous boundaries of old flat drawings." She said, "That's craft and you'll have to rejury." When I rejuried, I suddenly found myself a craftsman.

It was a period when I watched my friends have a much harder time selling the same drawings at art fairs that they had sold a few years ago very easily. Maybe people who have collected lots and lots of drawings have filled up their walls and now they're buying wedding gifts and bowls for their tables. The craftsmen are filling the places and enjoying the sales, and the artists are becoming more and more elite and exclusive. Friends of mine have had to face very big decisions. If they show at an art fair, they can't be in a gallery. You have to be exclusive. You can't be accessible. Whereas I have my things in very good crafts galleries, and they like me at the craft shows because it's PR for the shop. There should be galleries that show fine things by artistic people.

I started making clothing. Before I knew it, I found myself in one-of-a-kind clothing shows and sending off my work to some of the nicest exhibits in the country. I would read about them in the craft magazines. I'd send them pictures of my work and they would say, "Sure, we'd be glad to show your things." Wearable art is a different idea here in the Midwest. It's far more accepted in the East and on the West Coast. Clothing couldn't get into shows a couple of years ago. There's been more acceptance.

One show I entered was called The Enchanted Object. All the clothing accepted was clothing you could play with. I made a garden dress for my daughter. The pockets were filled with vegetables and the front had sunshine, and the back had a rainbow. Of course it was crazy. It was worth hundreds of dollars for all the work that went into it. The first reaction I'd get when I'd show it was, "Who'd pay $300 for a child's dress?" I didn't want to put a monetary value on it. I wanted people to look at it. Now people want to know more about how they can personalize their clothing to get that feeling. They don't want to follow the crowd. They don't want to buy it stamped out, or if they buy it stamped out, they want to add their little touch. Now they can appreciate what the craftsman does in having unique and special things. I operate this border between fashion and art.

When I heard that a manufacturer's representative was coming to town, I sent her a note and said I'd like to show her my things when she's in Chicago. She responded to the letter: Yes, she was interested. She looked at these things and said they were crazy. "I can't sell that. They show very well, but if you're going to put all that effort and all that money into a one-of-a-kind garment, my clientele buys silk." And then she said, "Look, I don't know anything about art, but I know fashion and I know what sells. Don't do this, do that." I had two choices. I could either be very independent and do my own thing or I could follow her advice. I followed her advice. I did one piece in silk. I followed her fashion tips. I wasn't compromising anything. It was simply, "Put it in this frame instead of that frame and you'll enjoy a better sale. This is what the decorators are showing this year." That's just called good business.

Instead of putting the soft sculpture on the garment where the lady feels sort of funny, if it's separate, she can take it off. If she's a little crazy, she can wear the soft sculpture either around her neck or around her waist as a belt. A lot of people would admire the soft sculpture and say, "I can't afford a couple of hundred dollars for a silk jacket, but I'd love the belt right now." And that's how a production business got started. The belts sold better than the jackets, or from one jacket I could sell several belts, although the belt was meant to be the accessory to the jacket.

I like the production pieces because they're a source of income. If I have paid for all my materials, then I can work on an exhibition piece without keeping track of my time, without worrying if it will sell. It's a far better piece than if I worry, will it sell? Should I skimp·on the materials? I can afford to buy a lot of silk, and then, once it's been paid for, I can just do what I please with it. With production work, however, there's a point where it's mindless, and it's not very important, and I want to do some important pieces. The other end of what I do is big silk wall hangings which are works of art. Somebody can buy them either to be made into blouses or to hang on the wall. I want to do the loftiest, finest things and not be tied down.

So far I've been talking about the creative end. There is a necessary business end to insure profitability or make the work worth the time. For me, the distasteful side of the craft business is bill collecting. Some retail businesses try to operate as long as possible without paying their bills. The rule of business is very simple: Keep putting bills to the back of the drawer and the ones that need to be paid, like electricity and phone, pay first, and keep putting off people who don't give you a hard time. The more I start kicking and giving a guy a hard time, the quicker he'll pay my bill and put somebody else off. If I'm quiet and meek about it, they keep shoving me to the back of the drawer. The reason I am very successful in collecting is they figure she's too much trouble, I'll pay her bill. Unfortunately this end also takes creative energy which I'd rather use in craft production.

I have been so used to dealing on a personal basis with personally made things that I take it very personally. I forget that this is just business and it's just a product and it doesn't mean a hooey to them. I now know how to ask for credit references. I know what to do for the first-time order until somebody establishes good credit with me. I take orders on a deposit basis.

Until recently, I would have accepted a big commission without having all papers in writing. Previously I had done a commission, not nearly as big as one I've just been commissioned to do, and worried and worried whether they would accept it. I'm delighted to have good friends who counsel me. The people at Mindscape Gallery, for example, tell me, "That was very clever of you to get the deposit and to get everything in writing. What did you provide for payments while the work is in progress?" On this new commission, I've asked as a stipulation to be paid one-third up front and a second third as the work is about two-thirds complete, and she agreed to it. If you've been paid as much as possible up front, you're not afraid of delivering the piece and waiting for the final payment. And at the same time, you're holding pieces of paper that say, "payment will be made within ten days of delivery, or requests for alterations must be made within ten days of delivery." Then you have every right to walk into court and say, "That guy accepted it. These were the terms and he has not fulfilled."[*]

Also, there are contracts that artists sign that they're entitled to 10% of any increase in value when the work is resold and the value has gone up. If I do commercial pieces, I know what rights I'm selling. I sign a contract when I create this piece that I'm signing away all rights. The buyer has the right to reproduce it, stick it on the cover of a book or magazine, pay me no royalties or royalties that we agree on. When I do a piece for the express purpose of reproduction in a book, I state all my terms up front. If I didn't, I could run into the problems that happened to an artist friend of mine. She had done a piece of art that the buyer wanted reproduced on his own Christmas cards, and then the buyer got it commercialized and sold it. My artist friend said, "Wait a minute. It was one thing to create it for your Christmas card for your own personal giving, but when you made money off it, I didn't know you were going to do that when I created this for you. I would have in-

---

[*]Subsequently I have learned there is such a thing as an installation clause. For example, an artist's final payment should not hinge on installation, only on delivery. Imagine a construction strike holding up the completion of a building for months. The artist's payment also would be held up for months.

sisted on rights." So there's deception involved. My artist friend is then placed in the position of proving intent. I have friends who will sell something and then be told, "We want to make sure that this is exclusive. Have you sold any other copies of this print? Where are they?" That's what's involved in buying rights. Of course there are many other aspects to the legal side of art. * Both artists and craftsmen need to acquaint themselves with sound business practices and their legal rights.

When you're brand new at it, you're not willing to be that assertive. You're desperate, and you're so anxious to be known, to be recognized, just to get your foot in the door, that you'll do anything and then beg for the money. You have to have confidence, and the only way you get it is repeated experience.

For information write: Sara Drower, 127 Laurel Avenue, Wilmette, Illinois 60091.

*Besides craft marketing seminars and a dozen books on the subject of legal rights, there is an association called Lawyers for the Creative Arts with branches in major cities throughout the United States.

Geri Willingham

STAINED GLASS DESIGNER AND FABRICATOR,
St. Petersburg, Florida.

About one-third of the artists and craftswomen we interviewed were skilled, educated technicians with at least a Bachelor of Arts degree. Whether or not their university education was completed, however, all the women agreed that the best way to learn technique in a craft is through serving an apprenticeship under a fine artist. Most home business artists, however, cannot afford to take on apprentices, especially in terms of teaching time.

Stained glass professionals, particularly today, should be encouraging apprenticeship. Everybody's starting to do stained glass now, and they're not doing it with any care. In the old days, people did nothing but stretch lead for two or three months. When they got through, they'd know how to do really fine craftsmanship. They'd be good. I've had people come in here and say, "Is there something you can tell me? I've read this book and I can't quite understand it, and I'm starting to teach a class tomorrow." Somebody actually called and said to me, "I've been asked to do this window that's going to be about 8′ × 10′. Do you think there's any need for me to worry about strength of the window?"

I did my undergraduate work at the University of Florida in Gainesville, and then I did a year of graduate work in painting in Hartford, Connecticut. Design and large mural work have always been a great interest.

I got into glass indirectly through the designing part of it. I was painting and sculpting in Seattle when a group began a stained glass firm and asked me if I would do the designing for them. They were doing lamps and small planters, and they wanted to do more windows, so I designed for them about a year. It was a new experience for me even though designing was my background. You have to determine, when you're doing the design work, the difficulties that are involved in cutting glass.

When they asked me to work for them, I was already planning to return to Florida because my Mom was still here. When I arrived back in Florida, I wasn't really sure exactly where I was going to locate, and in the meantime I began doing the glass work. I never got out of town.

While I was staying with my Mom, I was doing some glass pieces in an unbelievable little room that was like a large closet in the back of her place. I started getting orders and from doing shows I got more orders.

One show I did was a designers home show: 10 to 15 interior decorators each did a room in a very old home. I was asked by one of the designers who was doing the kitchen to make some stained glass panels for the kitchen windows, as well as some overhead lighting work. Orders resulted from the huge exposure of that show, and I started cranking out the work in this room of my Mom's that I could hardly turn around in. In time I had to decide whether or not to stay in St. Petersburg. Since I had orders to fill, I stayed.

Buying a home seemed more reasonable than renting because I knew I'd have to knock out some walls. I wanted a place in which I could work and live for two reasons: economy and safety. My hours are continuous mostly, and although I looked at a lot of situations where garages would have been ideal, I would have ended up going from a house to a garage late at night. I started looking for a house that had a work area connected to it. It wasn't easy to find just the right place because Florida houses generally have low ceilings.

It was unbelievably difficult for me as a single woman artist to get a bank loan. I had absolutely no capital. I spent months and months going from bank to bank. I looked like the worst possible risk because I had no assured income and I was alone.

One young real estate salesman was excited about what I was doing, and he projected that to a woman who happened to own this place. She was also involved in art and was sympathetic to what I was about to try to do. We had a private contract between us in which I made payments to her and she made her own payments to the bank. She agreed that as long as I made my payments, she'd hang in there with me. She was very enthusiastic and helpful — helpful, to say the least, because I was in a *place*! I was very excited about the fact that the house had a connected garage. After two and a half years, I was in good shape financially and had a better reception from one of the banks here in town. It was very encouraging for me then to be able to assume the mortgage on my own.

Glass is a very expensive medium. The larger the quantity you buy, the more you save, but to have the kind of palette I need, I must have a huge inventory of glass, and not just from one company. Of course, the larger the selection, the more exciting it becomes because of the greater freedom. I have a great amount of money invested, not just in glass, but also in lead, because I sell both to others working in glass. I want eventually to phase out of that. I'm only doing that in the same way that I was doing shows, in order to get to where I'm able to survive without it.

A problem that I have as a person working out of my house is that when the glass is shipped and the truckers see that there's no loading dock and no storefront, they're real uptight about it. Instead of pulling into my driveway, a truck driver, if he happens to be arrogant, will say, "I'm going to leave this shipment right here on the street. This is a private residence. I'm not going to bring it into your house," and one driver dropped it right at the end of the driveway. We're talking about 400 pounds minimum per crate when I get a full load.

Except for delivery problems and getting enough quality glass, my business provides me with a real sense of fulfillment. I can't tell you how lucky I feel that 95% of my commission work is my own design. In very few instances do I have to make any compromises. People come to me with an attitude that surprises me. For instance, a woman came to me and said, "We're building a new house. It's still in the very early stages," and I said, "Thank God! You didn't wait until it was time to say, 'What can I stick on this wall?' " It's my thing to make the pieces work in an environment, but only the same way that I'd want a piece of sculpture to work compositionally. The scope is larger, that's all. When I go out while the workmen are still putting in the foundation, I can feel the possibilities, and I did two windows that fit in environmentally. In that case, the woman ordered another window later.

I feel really good about satisfying myself first, but it's also important to me if I can do that and still satisfy the architect, the interior designer, and the person who's living in the house. When it happens, it's like a miracle to me.

After a piece is designed, the cost factor is brought in. You cannot talk about size and give anybody a price. I can take 2 square feet and do a $50 panel or a $500 panel.

The pieces that I do on my own develop in the same way my paintings do. I have feelings about a space, I have feelings about growing, ideas that have to do with me. I just use glass as a medium the same way that I would if I wanted to do a painting about that idea.

I'm really interested in incorporating other materials with glass. I found an old door and restored it and put a window in it. In the center of the window was a beautiful piece of crochet embedded in the glass and then I took the design that was in the crocheted piece and duplicated the design with stained glass around it. The ways that glass can be used seem limitless to me.

The three-dimensional torso piece is done with two-dimensional flat glass. The three-dimensional round quality comes from how I put it together. I want to do some work where I'm blowing glass, bending glass, changing the shape of the flat glass so that then the actual form changes.

A peak in my whole experience of art was when I did a commissioned portrait of Woody Herman in stained glass. What he represents in our time truly shows up in the piece. I was asked by RCA, who recorded the live concert when my piece was presented to him, if they could use the panel on their album cover. They wanted the right to photograph it, and I was paid for it. After this I learned how you really need to know about copyrighting so you know how to ensure that you receive credit for your design whenever and wherever it appears. They paid me a flat fee, and by allowing them to photograph and reproduce it, I opened it to the world to use. I didn't know that at the time. What followed was that another record company came along, and they wanted to do a larger blowup of it, and they didn't ask me. I just walked into a store and found it on the album cover. Right after that came the T-shirt people who have my piece centered on the front of the T-shirts they're selling, and there was nothing I could do about that. That was followed by posters made to promote his world tour. His manager, just out of niceness, sent me a couple of huge posters. There's no sign of the designer's name on them anywhere.

Woody Herman had a concert two weeks ago in Tampa, and now all the music stands have photos of my piece on them. When I walked into the concert, it just blew me away. Here's the entire band with my design in front of them, and the brochures and all the concert programs, everything had that piece on the front of it. I have to say that Mr. Herman's reaction to that piece was so beautiful and so meaningful to me and to him that even though I should have received monetary compensation and/or credit for having designed the piece, it was a really great experience.

Later that year, through an individual fellowship granted through the Fine Arts Council of the Florida Department of State, with assistance from the National Endowment for the Arts, Geri designed a stained glass sculpture fountain commemorating the ocean racing yacht. Geri wrote us:

The sculpture fountain was a huge undertaking. Besides the designing considerations for an outside terrace, I had to research water pumps and design and build the 4' x 8' copper base. I never could have started such a piece without the help of the state fellowship. I'm excited about the results, but tired at the moment and way behind on my commission work.

Kristin Anderson

ARTIST, ENAMELIST, AND METALSMITH,
Madison, Wisconsin.

*Three of the 26 craftswomen interviewed had no secondary income
as backup support and made the commitment to support themselves
solely through their craft work. It was a terrific struggle for all three of
them. Kristin accepted it while remaining philosophical.*

Every time I deviated from this path, circumstances have brought
me back to it again. It feels appropriate but not comfortable. I am
happy, if we assume that happiness is a goal, but I regard it as more
the result of a process than as a goal. That's not to say I don't get
unhappy. Constant tensions and anxieties are part of life, too. Like I
say, so much is appropriate and so much of what's happening is exactly what should be happening. A goal can be a limit, too, and I
really want to try to avoid setting myself up for limits.

This business resulted largely from my desire not to do what I didn't want to do. So many of the options that I saw were extremely unappealing to me, and then, through a conjunction of circumstances, this house became available to me, and that was really the precipitant for my thinking of myself as a business person—that I would make my living from my studio rather than from teaching or retailing or merchandising in some manner. Those were some of the other things that I had thought about.

I learned enameling by working as an enamelist on the production line in a factory in Norway. It was a very rough period, but one learns things that way. When I came back here again, I went to art school at the University of Wisconsin and began to think of myself primarily as an artist.

I'm the only artist-metalsmith in this area that I know about who is completely studio dependent, but I wasn't really in business for several years. A part-time teaching job at the vocational school was my main source of support. When I finished my degree in 1974, I started to look at myself much more in terms of business.

After I quit my job three years ago, I had no structure. Up to that time, I'd been in school, or I'd been working, or there had been some outside imposed structure on my life. When I quit my job, I had nothing, which on the one hand was fantastic and on the other hand was an absolute disaster. I decided I'd better pull together somehow and figure out how to avoid frittering. As soon as I try to impose something on myself, however, or somebody tries to impose something on me, I automatically go into a revolt, which is probably childish and certainly not admirable, but then I guess part of it is just learning to accept how one functions.

I decided how much I could make out of my studio, so I set an arbitrary figure of what I wanted to gross per month, and then I went backward from that, and it came out that I'd have to work 15 bench hours a week, and I thought, "Jesus! If you can't do 15 hours a week, you'd better go get a job!" So I put up a calendar at the head of my basement stairs to function like a time clock or guide, and my minimum for each week is to do 15 hours—any hours at all—actually making something at the bench in the studio. That doesn't include drawing time, thinking, or reading, and it doesn't include paperwork, interviewing, or marketing. Unless there are bench hours occurring, nothing else matters, and that has worked pretty well for me. It allows me flexibility but still gives me a measure. Last year it came to an average of 20 bench hours a week.

Every once in a while, people approach me about their being an apprentice and I say, "Great! You pay me." It would be nice to have somebody do a lot of automatic things, but if that's all they were doing, they'd go nuts—if they had intelligence and creativity themselves. By the time they were useful to me, they'd want to leave.

Every once in a while, too, I think about hiring somebody to do a lot of the production work, but then I'd have to redesign a lot of the pieces. I've had people try to cut out my patterns. Handling some of the tools is sort of like handling a pen, and every person's hand looks different. I don't want to be an administrator. I try to spend as little time as possible administering my life. It's another thing trying to think of somebody else.

My life is fairly simple, especially compared to that of most other women. I'm single and my only dependents have four legs, which means that I don't suffer from the child-related guilt feelings other women tell me about. I think that guilt feelings are counter-productive and best done away with, but that doesn't mean a person can just do that. I try to concentrate on feeling good as much as possible and on deliberately avoiding feeling bad. I also believe strongly that how I feel is largely up to me, which isn't to say that other people don't help or hinder but that if I foresee a situation that is going to be upsetting, I have various options in how to face it, only one of which is getting upset and feeling guilty.

I market my work primarily through art fairs. I also sometimes wholesale things and have dealt through galleries to some extent, but most of my income comes from my own direct sales. I aim for juried art fairs that are exhibitions as well as opportunities to sell, and I often get prize money at a fair. I don't mind if I don't sell a lot outright, especially if I get responses later on. A lot of people who consider buying a $250 piece want to think about it for a while, and they call me up later.

Various fairs have different reputations among artists as well as among the public. At one fair I attended the quality of the work was magnificent but the people weren't expecting the prices, and they were offended. Because they had a bargain-basement attitude I stopped going, but a couple of years later I went back and was absolutely amazed at the change in attitude of the public. I sold a $500 piece at that fair.

My pieces are designed to sell at various price ranges. Little enamels go for $50, $75, and $100 (1979 prices), but I price some things at under $50. Even people who don't make very much money can afford pieces at that level. They're my production models, my bread and butter, and I reproduce them as long as I feel like it. I also reproduce some pieces priced at $100 or more, but the price goes up $100 every time I reproduce it. I already have more sales for the little things than I can make—even for the things in the low hundreds. I have the option of starting a factory somewhere, but I'd rather design and create really developmental pieces, which then sell for $500, $800, $1,200, and up.

Since I got out of graduate school, I've been trying to get this whole situation pulled together—accumulating self-confidence, getting my base together so that I'm willing to take risks without completely devastating myself if something goes wrong.

If I'm doing whatever is the most important thing for me to do, everything else will work, but when my bank account is down to nothing, it's very hard. I really don't make enough money. And if I wanted to make money, I'd be doing something else. But it is important for me to make enough money doing this so that I can do it. I have a pipe dream—and who knows, maybe it isn't even a pipe dream either—of finding a patron some day. If I haven't done the primary work, the patron isn't going to be interested, so I've got to get that done. There's a constant conflict, a constant tension between doing what I call the money work and doing the art, and of course, to some extent, they're the same thing.

After the 1978 Chicago fair, I was almost sold out of all my little things, and with the Milwaukee fair coming up in two weeks I had a clear choice between getting one big piece finished for exhibition (and who knows, someone might even buy it) and getting little things done in order to meet my daily expenses. In that situation, I took the plunge and got the big one finished, but I sold very little because I had few of the little things to sell.

I put the bills in a pile, and when I get some money I sort them and say, Well, I've got to pay this one; I've got to pay that one; that one can wait. I used to get sick to my stomach about it, but I don't any more. The funny thing is, I very seldom get hassles and I seldom get duns. I do really try to keep on top.

I like business, and I like selling. There's an incredible high to selling even a little piece—and to sell a $500 or $1,200 piece at an art fair is just amazing! People imagine that you sell only little stuff at art fairs, but that's not true.

All of my work develops out of myself. I don't stock bracelets because I don't wear them, but if someone wants me to make a bracelet, sure, I'll make one. And since I have long hair and I wear hair pieces, I do make them, though not so very much on risk.

My larger pieces function like paintings, and because I regard the chest area as a good display place for paintings, I do a lot of pendants.

Since I wear pins to hold a cape closed, all my pins tend to be very large and heavy and when people say, "I can't wear that in my silk blouse," I agree. But I'm not interested in making pins for silk blouses unless some other thing is involved with them.

My large pieces have to do with meaning, which I regard as one of the functions of art. I like the idea of wearing things with meaning, which is how the personal talisman originated.

The few dreams I remember are very vivid, and the personal talisman I wear was a dream image from a time when I was extremely troubled. I remember thinking, "I don't know what this means, but I'm sure that it's important, especially since I've actually remembered it." It seemed like a signal: Pay attention to this! Remember this! This is important for you and how you function. In the course of my sketching it, it changed and developed and I began to see other things happening. I've redrawn it a couple of times in the last few years, so it continues to change, but its basic meaning is still there for me.

It's so easy to get distracted and forget things, but the talisman reminds me of things that I regard as important. I wear it all the time, partly so I know where it is and partly just to keep in touch. And of course, people ask me about it. Several people have asked me to do something like that for them, so I decided to put the talisman together as a marketable idea. When I'm commissioned to create a personal talisman for someone, we discuss his or her personal philosophy and things the person regards as important. After the person approves the design for the piece, I go ahead and create it. I hope it will be a total win for everybody—my coming into service in a very profound way and making my living at it, too.

For information write: Kristin Anderson, 2215 Kendall Avenue, Madison, Wisconsin 53705.

Carol Schwartzott

DESIGNER AND FABRICATOR
OF HANDWOVEN WALL FORMS,
Niagara Falls, New York.

Half of the 26 craftswomen we interviewed could support themselves through their craft work, although all but three of them had a secondary source of income — either husband's earnings or alimony. Those who manufactured and went into mass marketing brought in the most income.

Professionally run craft fairs can lead to manufacturing opportunities. In the early 1970s, Carol began to participate in the Rhinebeck, New York, Craft Fair, one of the top craft fairs in the country. Besides being a featured craftswoman, she has been a juror for the fair and so is able to discuss fair participation as a participant as well as from a juror's unique perspective.

My business began as an extension of a hobby. I taught school and saved up my money to buy a loom. I then spent two years experimenting with weaving in my own way, as well as doing graduate work in anthropology and textiles. I went to the library just about every free day I had and studied the American Indian and pre-Columbian cultures and their textiles, such as Central American Indian and Navaho tapestries and rugs. What evolved in my work came from that really intensive study.

A very good friend of mine, who had opened a craft shop in Buffalo, called me and said, "I heard you're weaving, Carol. Are you interested in selling some pillows on consignment?" So I started weaving for her shop.

I joined an organization called Buffalo Craftsmen, and I exhibited in some of their shows. Through friends, I was made aware of a craft fair in Bennington which changed over to Rhinebeck in 1975. At that time you just had to apply, and you were automatically accepted if you applied early enough.

I sold $200 worth of pillows that first year at the fair. I was really excited because it was the first real capital that I had ever earned through my weaving. The following year, when I returned, I was asked to be a demonstrating craftsman and was given a very nice location. Before I had even set up, there were 15 buyers from shops wanting to buy my pillows and other things—macrame necklaces and belts, little handwoven pouches and pillows. I was just elated, to say the least. I made about $1,000 that year, which was unbelievable to me.

Crafts were just coming into being in 1971, and craft shops were booming. The 1960s had been a time when people were learning handicrafts, and now they just took root. As the craft shops multiplied, so did the craftsmen, and a great many craftsmen came out of universities. Instead of teaching or instead of getting involved with a regular 9-to-5 job, they wanted to make it on their own as self-employed craftsmen. Now there was a tremendous influx of people making application to the fair, so it no longer was 300 spaces and 300 craftsmen—it was 300 spaces and 1,500 craftsmen applying.

There had to be some kind of selection system that would make it fair and square for old craftsmen and new. Previous participation in the fair was not totally fair to the people who were new and whose work might be as good or better in quality.

It was decided that there should be a jury set up. The director of the craft fair selected a craftsman for every area of craft—one potter, one jeweler, one fiber person, one wood person, and one person who was the Northeast representative to the American Crafts Council—to jury the craft fair. The following year, 1975, the jury was elected by fellow craftsmen at the fair. I was very happy and pleased that I was asked to be on the jury.

We had 2,400 applicants and 500 spaces. Each applicant submits five slides, so the jury sees a cross-section of the artist's work. A number on the slides corresponds to the number given when the application is submitted. At no time do any of the jurors know whom that number belongs to. A card describing the work accompanies each slide.

Excellent slides help. A lot of people send slides that are so bad that it can't be determined what's happening in them. Some people send slides that do not relate to one another. The juror is thus given the impression that this person is so experimental in his field that he has five different styles, and this gives an impression of immaturity, and the juror tends not to select them.

It's very difficult to make decisions. Those jurying saw the slides twice through for each person in each craft area. Say for pottery, we'd see numbers 1 to 300 first and then the reverse from 300 to 1. After a while, it became very monotonous and one looked like the other. When you see 600 slides of pottery times 5, you tend to get a little dizzy. Since I was not aware of how well-crafted an object was, I judged primarily on design—essentially what I *felt* was well designed. I'm very opinionated, and I found that my opinion changed very little from my original selection. Because I've got friends who were juried out who are good craftsmen, I'm sure it really boils down to a question of personal taste as far as the jury's concerned.

The fairs started becoming more and more hard sell, more and more businesslike. Now when you go to the craft fair, craftsmen wear suits when they're selling their craft. Their displays are slick, and sometimes you can't tell a handcrafted item from a commercial item, it's so well done. Prices have tripled and quadrupled.

Rhinebeck is still an excellent place to go because not only do you make sales there to the public, you make good contacts. You're getting museum directors going there to line up shows, so for someone with my interest, who hopes eventually to do commission work and museum shows only, it's good for building a network.

I met a man there from New York City who is in the Design and Decorator Building, which handles many of the interior decorators in the metropolitan area, and he started representing my work. We decided the next step would be to contact interior designers and decorators across the country, and we mailed them a pillow brochure. But it didn't work. My work has to be seen in order to be bought.

Then we met and made friends with a guy who is an architect from up the road here about 20 miles and we got to talking. He had ideas of representing me and selling my work across the United States and the idea was to get a brochure together for that. We worked and worked on it. It took two years before we got the brochure together. First we couldn't find someone to photograph the things properly. The original photographer who had done such a beautiful job photographing the pillows died of a heart attack. We used four different photographers before we were able to get the catalogue together properly illustrating the hangings. We mailed it out and again it was no go. We got two or three orders and that was it.

The representative in New York City agreed that people had to see my work in order to buy it. He said he'd be my worldwide representative if I'd give him an exclusive. I was going to make all kinds of money. "How many things can you weave?" he asked. He was going to set me up with representatives in each major marketing area—one each in California, Los Angeles, Chicago, High Point, North Carolina (the furniture area of the United States), Texas, and his own in New York. These representatives were going to sell to all the interior designers and decorators within their areas and the business was going to mushroom. Right?

I ended up not getting paid. When I went to call up Mr. X in New York, he was in Milan at the furniture show for a month, then he was in Greece for a month, in Israel for a month. I could never contact him for the overdue accounts, and I got madder and madder. Then I got a letter from the California representative who said that Mr. X had told him this was consignment work and that he wasn't going to pay me, and if I wanted to get paid, he'd ship my things back. Finally Mr. X came back from Europe and I called him up, and he said, "Oh! I'll get in touch with them and I'll tell them . . . " — and at last I got paid. We didn't get any reorders from his accounts and so I decided to drop him.

Well, I said to Peter, my husband, I can mark back down my work, take the 20% off from the representative's fee, mark the modulars and the hangings and the pillows back down to the prices that they were and sell more because when you triple the price, it adds up. New York designers take my price of, say, $100 and they put a price tag of $300 on it in the showroom. When a decorator comes in, they give her a third off, so she is paying full retail value for the piece. Then she, in turn, if she's not working on a fee for the job, marks it up another third to the client. So the client ends up paying three times the net price.

This year at the craft fair, again Mr. X sat down to discuss the plans for the coming year. My husband and I decided to give him an exclusive only in the New York metropolitan area, and I would keep all my other accounts (plus my established accounts within the New York area). I was also free to do shows and exhibits. We told him unless he starts giving us enough business, that's it for the exclusive.

It's difficult if you're nice. You have to be very firm. That's the only way that you can succeed, it seems. It's just like dealing with the craft shops. You send them an order and they're supposed to pay you in 30 days. Most of them take two or three or four months. You have to call them long distance, and you have to send three or four bills.

So even though this is a terrific business because of its flexibility — if the children get sick and I have to take a week and nurse the kids, I can — it's also got its bad points. I don't get that paycheck coming in steadily every week, and I have to worry about getting paid. I don't know what I can do about it except go through representatives and then put up with the problems I have with them.

My business is more and more geared toward the wall rather than the sofa. When I started weaving, it was pillows, because they were easily produced and I had a production line. I even hired a girl who worked for me two years full time. But all my profit went to paying her salary, and I just couldn't afford her. I was working just as hard as I was when she was not with me, and I was making less than a third of the net proceeds. I've tried to eliminate the smaller, less expensive items and get into the larger, more expensive ones so that I can sell less and make more money.

I can see my business developing to the point where an architect will come in and say, "I have a 400-room apartment complex going up and need fiber for 200 of those rooms which we're going to rent"; or I can see my work as large-scale pieces for entry halls and reception areas where 15′ × 40′ tapestries are needed. I'm tired of producing the smaller modular that fits into a home setting. I want to get out of the residential and into the commercial setting.

A year later Carol told us:

It's finally starting to happen. The New York representative and I have both mellowed together, and we realize we need each other. Now he's giving me topnotch service. I'm doing very few pillows and am concentrating on residential wall hangings. Recently I got my first commercial commission, a 5′ × 9′ wall hanging for Republic Steel for their combined conference and executive dining room.

For information write: Carol Schwartzott, 633 Buffalo Avenue, Niagara Falls, New York 14303.

Ferne Williams

MANUFACTURER, PEDDLER, WHOLESALER, MAIL ORDER BUSINESS OWNER, West Orange, New Jersey.

Creating sufficient inventory and selling in volume are the most essential factors of a successful home manufacturing business. Low overhead costs permit home business owners more readily to self-finance and increase volume as the business expands.

My business developed as I went along, and when I added up last year's gross, it came to $52,000, which amazed me. I make 95% of what I sell, and I was amazed that I had produced and sold that volume, because all I make depends on impulse buying. People don't need the things I make.

In 1974 I became separated and, shortly thereafter, divorced. I had four children: 21 and 19 and two who were 17. I really didn't know what I was going to do. I had never thought about the fact that, first of all, I would be divorced and, second, that I would have to earn a living and support myself. It was never in my head because when I was married and the children were growing up, I was doing what was expected of me. I never, ever thought of divorce.

At various times during the marriage, I worked. I took odd jobs just because I found that, by working outside of the home, I felt better. My mother used to kid me because I used the money to buy my own clothes. She said, "Why don't you put it in the bank?" and I said, "No. It gives me a real good feeling to know that I'm earning the money for the clothes that I'm buying." And she said, "Well, why save it for his next wife?" and I said, "Ha! Ha!" It was just nothing that I thought would ever happen.

I realized that I was going to have to make a living when I discovered that the little bit of "back pay" called alimony was not going to enable me to pay bills and live in my present location. I thought about going back to school since I didn't have a college degree, but I'm not a student. I've always been mechanically oriented, and through the years I learned all kinds of crafts and I realized there were quite a lot of things that I could do.

I thought about going into a small appliance repairs business because I felt that some women might want a woman rather than a man to come into their homes to repair a television set or a toaster or refrigerator or do electrical work, but I realized I'm not as young as I was. Some of those jobs are physically difficult, and even though I'm in good shape, as I get older it would get harder and harder.

In 1970 when I had joined the local NOW chapter, they needed someone to do fund raising for them, so I had opened a small boutique. At home, I made such things as jewelry and bumper stickers and note paper, which women bought and which made our NOW chapter a profit. After my divorce, I continued making those things and my business evolved.

My folks helped me buy my ex-husband's half of this home. Alimony provided my start-up capital, which basically paid for the mortgage and the heat. I didn't need to have a huge amount of capital because I had a place to live. I didn't need money to buy anything except food and to pay for anything except my current bills. I would buy a small amount of merchandise and sell it and use that profit to buy more. Then I expanded.

I started with note cards and jewelry. I would silk screen each note card separately. I have lines in the cellar, and I'd hang each card up to dry. I would buy baggies and stick a dozen in and sell them. The first jewelry I made was the women's equality symbol, and then I found a lot of women didn't want it. They wanted the plain biological symbol, instead. Gradually I expanded.

Most of the things I sell have slogans; they have a meaning and they're for consciousness-raising. I have to find people who will design the things for me, then I manufacture them. I began with only three button slogans. Now I have close to a hundred. Originally I had one of those little hand machines, and I would sit and make buttons. I sell close to 300,000 buttons a year, and so now I have a manufacturer who makes them for me.

I sell most of my merchandise at conferences or on street corners. I'm a peddler. Many times when I'm walking on the streets, I say, "Ferne, where have you come from? What are you doing?" It's a whole change that I have to do in my head to say, "It's O.K. You can be a peddler. You can stand out on the corner."

I find that sometimes I don't have the nerve to peddle. I'll stand there and feel very embarrassed, so I'll close up and go home. Other times I feel very strong and I can stand there because I don't get too many people who criticize. The criticism is by the antifeminists and focuses mainly on the various slogans. I try not to argue or discuss because it develops into a hassle and turns customers away. Remember, I'm there to make money.

Men sometimes buy things as a joke. Women buy more because it's serious to them. It's not just in the feminist arena that my items sell. For instance, I have these slogans, too: "Children Are People Too," and "Cancer Cures Smoking," and "How Dare You Presume I'd Rather Be Thin!"

When I was standing outside the Democratic Convention on a corner in New York City opposite Madison Square Garden, I was just mobbed all day long. I was there for three days. I got a ticket the last day because I didn't have a peddler's license. A City of New York statute says if you're selling political items, you don't have to have a peddler's license, so I went into court and my ticket was dismissed. After that, I got a license, but I found that it didn't do me any good, anyway, because selling in the City of New York is restricted in practically all places. You can still chance it, and I do.

I started in mail order last year. The most exciting part of my day is going down to my post office box and getting the mail because I'm getting responses from the ads that I run in *Ms.* magazine and other periodicals. I look at the orders for the day and maybe for the day before, and I'll go downstairs and start producing the items that I need to mail out.

I try to make all the T-shirts I need for one particular slogan and then hang them up to dry. I don't like the repetition in my work— say, making one hundred tote bags: laying out the fabric, marking it off, cutting it out, taking the pieces downstairs to the screening room, screening them, hanging them up to dry overnight, taking them back upstairs the next morning, and sewing them up. Sometimes the work gets so monotonous that I go from one thing to another. I might go outside and paint the house or change the oil in the car.

Some days I go into New York City or other places where I buy the raw goods of whatever it is I have to make: clothing items such as T-shirts, jogging shorts, sweat shirts, nightshirts, raincoats; fabric for tote bags; everything that goes along with the jewelry — various metals such as silver and gold, chains, etc. —and paper for the note cards and bumper stickers.

It's very exciting when I go to conferences and get reassurance that, yes, women do like the things. They praise what I make and they say, "My goodness! How can you make all these things?" It's because I work from morning to night making things.

To go to a conference without a lot of stock is horrendous. I always make more things than I need so that I have enough. I don't too often get stuck because if something doesn't sell at one conference it will sell at another or I can always use it for the mail order business.

International Women's Year was a big year and there were conferences in various states. I wasn't allowed to sell at most of the state conferences, even in my own state, so I was out on the lawn hanging things from my van and laying things on the grass and getting massacred by people who just couldn't get the stuff fast enough. Luckily another friend came along and helped me. You have to look for sizes and colors and refill the button box. You have to queue people up if they are fighting to buy things. Sometimes I feel as if I might literally pass out I'm under such strain.

Each time I go to a conference, I don't know where I'm going to be physically located. I don't know where people are going to walk in, or where they're going to come out. It's a totally new situation every time I go. Even when I know that I have a table space, I don't know if I'm going to have a wall space in the back to hang up the things to show. How can people see all the things I have? I have to devise a way to get the merchandise shown so that they can just stand there and see it. I have to be totally prepared to sell for a whole day, which means I have to bring everything: food, something to drink, something to sit down on, a table, a tablecloth, bags to put merchandise in, a mirror so people can see how the jewelry looks, and a suggestion box for slogans or anything else they might like to have.

I have a red VW van with a bed in the back. I go to any kind of conference attended by males or females that will allow me to have a table and sell my things: psychology conferences, teacher conferences, etc. I can very definitely take enough merchandise with me to sell and make the trip worthwhile, and I find the things that I make sell to everyone. I don't have to make special products for the different conventions.

As I get older, I realize that physically it's very difficult going to the music festival in Wisconsin, or to the Women's Law Conference in Atlanta, and then to the International Women's Year Conference in Texas. I did it and I intend to continue to do it, but I can see where it's getting more difficult.

Because a lot of people who come to the conferences are the same ones year after year, I have to have new things, and that's why I went into things for the office. There are different kinds of plaques on the walls of offices which are "Ha! Ha!" okay, but we have to start raising people's consciousness to such harmful customs as calling women "girls." A lot of women don't mind being called a girl, but they certainly don't call their bosses, who are usually men, boys. There is definitely a difference between a man and a girl in people's heads. If you go into an office and the women are all "girls" and the bosses are men, you know how the pay goes.

I cannot get up and make speeches like some other women and I can't write books, but I feel that I'm providing a service. The things that I make are helping to raise people's consciousness, and so I really feel I'm helping the movement.

I wondered how long this could keep going. How long will feminists or women have meetings? How long will they want to wear T-shirts? I got scared, and so I went to the Small Business Administration and asked for some advice as to what type of business they thought I should go into. They suggested a service-oriented business.

They felt I would be good at it. I wrote a letter to my brother and I voiced the same fears, and he said that he thought I should stay with it and do the things that I knew the most about. Shortly thereafter, my business started to grow. I realize now that I must have been at a turning point.

I'm now selling a lot of my things wholesale to stores around the country, and thank goodness for that because there are not that many conferences all the time. One of the biggest problems is where is a conference being held? When? Will they in fact let me sell? Sometimes they won't. Now that I have the mail order business started and am selling wholesale to stores, I'm not as concerned with having to go to the conferences because I realize I can make money wholesaling.

Still, even now I never know how much I'm going to make or even if I'm going to make it. It's all so iffy. I really never know what's going to happen, and I get fearful every once in a while. Another worry that I have now is how can I grow? There's only so much I can do with my own hands during a day. I work all day all the time. And if I should grow larger, I still have the stress that every other business has—going month to month, not really knowing if there's going to be any business. I'm concerned about earning a living.

For product information write: Ferne, P.O. Box 113, T.C.B., West Orange, N.J. 07052.

SHOEMAKING

There are 8 essential Steps

1 Pouring plaster of Paris mold.
2 Tearing the old Shoe apart.
3 Making permanent Cardboard patterns.
4 Cutting patterns out of Fabric.
5 Making a sample for Practice.
6 Sewing the shoe upper onto the mold.
7 Removing the shoe upper from the mold.
8 Completing the gluing Process.

SIMPLE, UNSOPHISTICATED TOOLS

Faa Casper

TAILOR, SEAMSTRESS, AND SHOEMAKING TEACHER,
Milwaukie, Oregon.

Sewing skills were used by more than half of the craftswomen and about one-fifth of all the women we interviewed. Sometimes these businesses were geared toward providing supplemental income, while at other times they provided the total support for the family.

First I made my children's clothes. That was part of the contribution to the family budget. The fact is, when I bought my sewing machine, it was terribly expensive for us because we were going to school, but I needed a new machine. In less than six months, through my sewing jobs, I had paid for my sewing machine, contributed to paying for the everyday expenses of our family, and helped my husband through school.

I did tailoring and seamstress work for faculty wives and other townspeople. I sewed costumes for the high school pep team and the baton twirlers. I even sewed for the community prostitutes. Oh, I tell you! They bought the most glamorous fabrics you can imagine. It was just a pleasure to sew that fabric. And I learned a completely new way of clothing construction — easy on, easy off. I'd have yards of that glamorous material left, and they were generous with tips. I really enjoyed sewing for them.

Faa expanded her sewing skills to include shoemaking, and then she developed a shoemaking course which has been approved by the Oregon Department of Education. Her students can receive credit through the home economics division of the community colleges through which she teaches.

My feet hurt. I got so tired of leaving my home in shoes and coming back carrying them that I decided to do something about it. I felt there had to be a way of making comfortable shoes. This has been a universal cry from women and men, but they just make do.

I decided that the logical way to start, since I knew nothing whatever about it, was to take the shoes apart and learn the processes. Any time that I found someone who knew something about it — shoe repair people and others — I picked their brains.

A woman who advertised through the newspapers was conductting shoemaking classes through one of the craft shops here. She taught the principle of making a mold from a brand new pair of shoes. But if the new shoes didn't fit, there was no possibility of making a pair of shoes that fit by using her molds. I started from that point and developed the methods necessary to make that mold fit. It's all explained in a book that I've written (not yet published), and I cannot discuss it at this time.

The mold is very valuable. Your feet do not change as much as you think, but if they do change, you can take that mold and accommodate those changes very easily because you've learned the principle of making that mold fit, no matter what.

You sometimes will want to change the height of your heel. I'm not as agile as I used to be and I'm not as secure on my feet, so I have gone from higher heels to lower heels. Your molds cannot accommodate heel size varying more than ¼" for any particular mold, so you have to make your molds according to the heel height that you want.

I suggest to my students that they get a pair of shoes that are comfortable to wear. They may not fit totally, but the shoes that they start with should be more comfortable than anything else they've got. That's the beginning, but there's much more that we do to make them absolutely fit.

For instance, if a woman has a huge bunion on her foot, we make her a pair of shoes that accommodate that bunion but still look very new and very sharp. In one of my classes recently, I had a man who had one foot size 6½ and one foot size 9½. Even the shapes of his feet were different. We made molds for him that enabled him to make a beautiful pair of boots. He was just simply delighted because never had he had any comfort at all in shoes.

I've seen people who had the most miserably misshapen feet you can imagine, people who had gone through excruciating pain. They have not only gone out of my classes with comfortable shoes that they could wear but they could even go dancing again. One lady, in particular, had some of her toes shortened because they were so overlapped, and we made her comfortable shoes.

The simplicity of the tools really surprises people. My students have never had to buy anything other than a Stanley cutting tool or a carpet cutting tool or a curved fingernail scissors. Most of the tools needed can be found in kitchen drawers or in the tool chest.

Because of the simplicity of the tools I teach my students to use, I was challenged by the president of the Master Shoe Repair Association of Oregon. I was teaching my first class at the Mount Hood Community College and I received a letter from this man demanding that my classes be thrown out because I was misleading the public. It wasn't possible for simple unsophisticated tools to be used. I couldn't do what I was saying I could do when they had to spend thousands of dollars for their equipment in their shoe repair shops. He went on to say that I hadn't had any training in the legitimate schools.

A few days later I got a call from an absolute stranger, and she said, "Mrs. Casper, I've seen you on TV, I've heard about you for a long time, and I know that you know what you're doing. In the paper this horrible person has written a letter to the editor 'exposing you,' as he calls it, and really, it's a terrible letter. I want you to answer that!" And then I started getting calls from people that I've never heard of, telling me, "Don't let him get away with it!"

I got the paper and there was the letter: what a charlatan I was and how misled the public was and I was a downright liar. I waited for a few days thinking about it. I thought, I'm not going to react. I'm just going to maybe chide him a little.

So I wrote to the editor indicating that this person had perhaps leaped before he looked. He had never called me, he had never discussed with me or investigated whatever I was doing. I most certainly *was* teaching my class how to make shoes and we most certainly did use the tools that I said we were using. At the end, I just thought

I'd kind of nudge him a little and I said, "I think that this person is against free enterprise." I also said, "Where would the numbers of women who sew in their homes be today if the garment industry had taken the same stand as this person has? There would be no home seamstresses today."

A couple of days later I got a telephone call from this man, and he apologized and offered me an honorary membership in the union. I didn't accept it. Oh, I had a good time talking with him. We talked pretty plain. He said his wife was terribly angry at me for the letter that I had written because it really did put him down in a nice way. I had grounds to sue, but I didn't do it. I could have caused trouble and possibly collected, but from whom? He didn't have any money. Of course he was a spokesman for that union, but I wasn't interested in anything like that. I *was* interested in defending myself, though.

I've had communication from all over this nation and even from outside. The former Mrs. Moshe Dayan of Israel was promoting crafts among Israeli women and the Arabs, hoping that crafts would bring them closer together and erase some of the problems they were experiencing. I was contacted by a liaison man, but then something happened over there. One of their emergencies arose, and nothing else came of it. And at an International Conference for Homemakers and Crafts in Salt Lake City, the Japanese visitors were intensely interested in my shoes and in the demonstrations that I conducted. I noticed that they were at every single demonstration taking notes. I've had people invite me from Canada, back East, Texas, and California to come and conduct classes. I'd even have had my expenses paid and the classes set up for me, but I don't want to leave my husband, my seven children and 23 grandchildren.

I feel that I'm actually contributing to the economy of the nation, because America is no longer a shoemaking country. In ten years from now, according to the officials at the U.S. Labor Department, all of the shoes used in the United States will be imported. Almost all of them are now. I feel that teaching an individual how to make good looking, comfortable shoes inexpensively is a considerable contribution. Teaching classes is simply not a money-making situation; the total overview is the important thing.

Wilhelmine Fuhrer

TAX CONSULTANT AND PUBLIC ACCOUNTANT,
Auburn, Indiana.

Of the 14 women we interviewed who lived in rural areas, ten were engaged in product-oriented businesses. One of the four service-oriented businesses was Wilhelmine's 38-year-old accounting business which she ran from her farm 6 miles out of the nearest town — Auburn, Indiana, with a population of 7,337.

The traffic in and out of this office in a year's time is approximately 5,000. I do an average of 2,500 federal tax returns, and for each federal tax return I do a state return. Most of my clients book their appointments ahead of time. Right now, around 1,800 are already booked for this year.

I graduated from a secretarial program at a business college, and I did nothing but office work. I worked for a lumber company for nine years, and my employer taught me the fundamentals of filing tax returns. Then I worked for an insurance agent. My training was insufficient, so I wrote to the government and asked them to set up a tax school, which they did at the Claypool Hotel in Indianapolis. Ever since, I have gone to tax school prior to the tax season so that I know of the changes that have taken place in tax law the past year.

When we moved here, I had to work since we had just purchased our farm and were deeply in debt. I didn't believe in women working away from home if they had a family, so I ran a small ad in our local paper and put a sign in the window in my home that I was doing tax work.

I started out with 12 clients the first year. My aim was to double that the next year and have 24 clients, the next year to have 48, and so on until I built up my business. If someone moved or died whose return I had done the year before, I would try to replace him with a new client, and of course I eventually got to the point where I couldn't double my clients because there weren't enough hours in the day or enough days in the week.

Eventually I had to move my business out of my house because Internal Revenue kept increasing the number of tax forms and there was no place to put the additional paper. I still wanted to work from my home, however, so I decided to build an office building on land adjacent to our property. I had to go before the DeKalb County Planning Commission. I had to send letters to folks whose land joined my piece of property to ask them to come to a meeting if they opposed my putting up my office building. No one put up any objection whatsoever.

When I moved to the new building, costs skyrocketed because now my business was considered a commercial venture. I had to pay more for electricity and telephone, for example. Gradually my business increased to include clients from 18 states, so the number of forms my business required each year developed to the point where I had to put a 12' x 12' room onto the original building.

Besides the work I do in my office, for 33 years I've been doing tax returns in Amish homes. They don't have electricity, so I have to have manually operated adding machines and typewriters to do that work. This started when an Amish family moved in about 2½ miles from my home, and one day, after the father came to get his tax return done, he said, "I wish you would go down and see Mr. X at Grayville and tell him that I sent you." I felt skittish, but I did go down and contact Mr. X, who said he was very interested and that his neighbors would be, too. He set up appointments for them at definite times, and anyone who came five minutes late had to go to the end of the line and wait because he decided that no one should ever keep Mrs. Fuhrer waiting. His neighbors accepted it, and so it was quite a pleasure to go there and work.

I proved to them that keeping records meant that for each dollar they could account for and deduct (at that time 20¢ on the dollar), they could save 20¢. Thereafter they kept book records. Every year I taught them more until they learned to keep sufficient records for a government audit.

Through the years I've been involved in all kinds of things along financial lines, and it has come strictly from my clients' confidence that I'll be able to answer their questions. This last telephone call I had is a good example of that.

This gentleman feels free to call and discuss his problems with me and ask whether I think he is doing the right thing. He's a very conscientious person with four children, and he doesn't want to take anything away from them. He owns two farms and wondered if he should sell them and give a cash settlement to his ex-wife, who had suddenly left him. I said, "No, you're not going to want to stay in the factory all your life because you're not a factory man to start with. Don't do it that way." So we talked about it and decided which way to divide his property so that she got what he thought was her fair share and he'd still be situated all right.

Recently I had a heartbreaking experience. Until this year, I had always done the tax return of an Amish man whom I've known since he was a little boy, and I'm a good friend of his mother's. A few years back, he broke away from the Amish and went modern. He got married, built a new home and a business building where he manufactured plastic caps for pickup trucks. He had five full-time employees.

A year ago this last June, I called him and said, "I don't have your quarterly work and the information that I need to finish up your income tax computation for the year." "You don't have to worry about it," he said, "I'm a poverty case." That knocked me for a loop. I said, "A poverty case? How in the world are you a poverty case?" His gross had been over $250,000 a year. "Will you please come to my office. I must talk to you."

So he came up here and said, "I'm registered in the Recorder's Office at the Courthouse at Fort Wayne as a poverty case." Some religious cult from California had brainwashed him. He had deeded his home, his business building, his truck, his van, and his bank account to what is known as the LCS of Allen County. What LCS stands for, I have no idea. He said, "I'm not going to file a tax return. The organization is going to take care of that for me this year."

The tax attorney that we had at our Indiana Society of Public Accountants tax seminar this year mentioned that this kind of thing is happening and that we should be on the alert. I think it's the most tragic thing that I have been involved in here in the last year and I still am upset.

Every now and then I run into an individual who is so crooked that I refuse to sign his tax return. Internal Revenue has such strict rules and regulations that it can fine us for any misdemeanors that we might commit on our own, and if an accountant is knowingly involved in fraud he can be sentenced to jail or prison. This year, I'm sorry to say, the most fraudulent person I've dealt with is the minister of a church in Ohio some of whose parishioners are my clients. He came to this area with a sob story, and his parishioners felt sorry for him and built him a nice new house. They pay his utilities, they furnish his car, and he has a fixed amount of cash that he gets per week, but he told me that he doesn't have any income from the ministry because these are strictly gifts to him. He had sold a farm in Illinois for a lot of money and he gets between $3,000 and $4,000 a year in interest, yet he wouldn't designate one penny of income. If he has declared himself a minister and is affiliated with a church, naturally he's got to have income.

More typically, if I find clients overextended I tell them what to do to pay back their debts. If I'm keeping books for a small business, and I see it is going broke, for one reason or another, I take it upon myself to notify the owners of their specific shortcomings. Many of these small businesses don't have a profit-and-loss statement each month. The only thing they know is that they have X dollars in their checking account to pay their bills, or if they don't have anything there they don't know why. I tell them they must change this or that in order to remain in business.

I try to do a good job, to give my clients service, to take the time to discuss their problems with them individually and not run them though like a computer. One of my clients told me this week, "We always feel welcome in your office. If we have a question, we know you will take time to either answer it or get the answer for us. On top of that, you don't charge us each and every time we ask you a question. All those things have meant a great deal to us."

Wilhelmine's three children have now grown and moved off the farm. Her husband has retired from his job in Fort Wayne, and the farm is mostly rented. Still, Wilhelmine continues her accounting practice. Early in 1978 she decided to undergo a cataract operation to rejuvenate her failing eyesight. After the operation the surgeon informed her that he had removed one of her eyes. After nearly four decades of building up and servicing her clients, she must now cut back her list of clients to preserve her remaining sight.

Some folks have been with me all these years. Most of them book their appointments a year ahead of time. But I'm going to have to start cutting out some. How do I pick the ones to tell that I won't do their tax returns this coming year because I lost an eye?

The first thing I'm going to do is notify all my Amish clients, except those who come to the office, that I will no longer be traveling to them because I cannot do tax returns by kerosene light for 12 to 14 hours. Physically I feel as good as I did last year, but I have to make some changes in order to save my remaining sight.

Karen Davies

MANUFACTURER OF AUTHENTIC COSTUMES
FOR ANTIQUE DOLLS
Issaquah, Washington.

Many home businesses specialize is esoteric products and services, consequently their markets are narrow and can be reached only through very specific networks. Ranging in price from $25 to $65, Karen's costumes for antique dolls are sold to women who are in the antique doll business and to women who compete their dolls at conventions.

Seven years ago my mother was starting to sew doll clothes for needy children, and she asked me if I would be willing to help her get things ready for Christmas time. Since I do like to sew, it struck my fancy right away, so I helped her assemble as many as I could. We started in October, and by Christmas we had completed 80 dolls between the two of us. The following year, we completed 150 costumes and the third year we completed 200. It was that third year when a couple of older ladies from our church asked if I would be willing to make doll dresses for some old-fashioned dolls they had. I had never even seen an old-fashioned doll except maybe once or twice in a museum. I was amazed that people had them.

These dolls struck a real interest with my mother as well as myself, and since we were still working on our Christmas project for needy children, she ran an ad in the newspaper that read something like this:

Wanted. Old dolls. Any kind. Any condition. To
be used for children at Christmas time.

She got several responses. One lady came in with an old-fashioned bisque doll head. The body had long since been broken and discarded and she said, "Just take it." When I saw it, I thought it was so unique that I looked up *doll hospitals* in the Seattle phone book and, to my amazement, I found one. They were not able to match the head with a body, but I couldn't believe all the fabulous old dolls I saw for sale there.

I came home so excited and I told my husband all about the new doll interest. I said, "They're more than just dolls. They're part of the history of children's antiques." I also told him about the prices that went along with these little treasures. He told me right then that if I thought I wanted any of them, I was going to have to arrange my own finances, but he didn't want me working outside of my home. He felt that a lady's place, when she has any children, should be at home if possible, I had once worked as a keypunch operator, but now I was at home with my 12-year-old son. So I had a twofold problem. Number one, I wanted the treasures that cost so much, and number two, I had no way to get them because I couldn't work outside of my home.

I decided that I'd ask around to see if there were any people who needed to have any doll clothes made. I had noticed that in the doll hospital there were several dolls that were not dressed. I said, "Well, do you dress these, too?" And she said, "Sometimes but not usually." She didn't know of anybody that did this. I thought, "'Well, then. Why not me.?"

I inquired around a little further and I found in another small outlying town a lady who made antique doll appraisals. I went to see her collection of dolls, and she told me about a group of ladies in Seattle that were getting together to start a club of antique doll collectors. I thought, "Although it sounds ridiculous, I'll go, and maybe there will be somebody there that needs some doll clothes."

I went to observe the other people buying the dolls, and thought maybe I could dress the dolls that they were able to buy. It was the second time that this group of women had met, and they were in the process of electing officers. They wanted to group together and become an organized club to study antique dolls, where they came from, who made them, what were their dates, how did they get here, and who had them. I walked out that afternoon as president of a new club.

At the next meeting, I told them that my main interest was not only the dolls, but costuming of dolls, and several of them were very glad for that, because they could not sew a stitch. That was ideal for me so I started there.

The first year I did it on a casual basis. Sometimes a person would say, "Well, I have three or four dolls I'd like to have costumed. Could I give you an old doll in trade instead of paying you money?" And of course I thought that that was ideal, too, because I didn't have to pay a dime. All I had to do was spend a few hours to costume their dolls.

After that, the person who took home the dolls that I had dressed showed them to other collector friends of hers and, the next thing I knew, I was busy most of my spare time.

I am quite busy in my church and at my son's school, and I garden, and the inside takes a minimum amount of care no matter how you look at it. But whenever I had spare time, I'd race down to my laundry room where I had my sewing machine at the time, and I would sew, sew, sew.

I had no patterns. The people had a picture with them and they said, "Can you make something like this?" The modern patterns and the old patterns really aren't that similar. I was starting to draft a lot of my own patterns, making them up as I went. I had by now been sewing the best part of the year off and on. I had done five or six costumes, and I went to the library and checked out a whole stack of books on antique clothes and antique dolls—everything that had to do with costume and turn-of-the-century toys and children's and ladies' wear. I came home and I read and read, and the more I read the more I became interested in clothing generally, as well as in antique dolls and their costumes.

As I was sewing for the antique dolls, I started looking all over for old fabrics. I'd go into antique shops and second-hand stores, and I'd ask for old lace and old fabric. I started coming across some antique clothing tops, turn-of-the-century ladies' bodice things that you see hanging around the room here, and I thought, "There's no way I'm going to cut those up to make a doll dress. I'll search further for my fabric for the doll clothes. I'm going to buy a collection of costumes because they are history in themselves." I just couldn't put my scissors to them.

About this time, a friend of mine said, "I'm subscribing to a booklet on antique dolls and related items that is published back in Michigan, and you can place a free ad." That was the first advertising I did, and it cost me $8 for the year to subscribe. In it they had dolls and carriages, and now my doll clothes for sale. As I was reading my first issue, I got a call from Virginia from a lady who said, "I would like to place an order." I told her how much it would cost her and how long it would take her until the delivery was made to her. After she received her order, she wrote back that she went to all the conventions on the East Coast and had a shop in which she sold antique furniture and expensive doll-related items. She wanted to do consignment items, and she was very confident that what I was doing would sell very well. So I sent her a shipment of a dozen costumes, and she sold them out of her shop before she got them to the convention. She called back and said, "Please send me more as quick as you can." This was November 1976. I thought, "It's the Christmas rush. I'll make all I can before Christmas time." I found I was averaging over $10 an hour. I told my husband, and he said, "How about it!" and he encouraged me to start putting in a little more time.

Christmas came and the lady from Virginia was going to some New York conventions and people in the Seattle area also wanted items, and I found that I couldn't keep up. So I called a very good friend who did sewing very similar to what I did and asked her if she would be interested in sewing costumes, which I'd buy outright from her for redistribution. She *was* interested, and now I buy from her wholesale. I decided to concentrate *all* my time in sewing. I could see that there was starting to be a lot of money and a lot of demand for this kind of thing.

January and February went by with flying colors, and I was still averaging, without leaving my room here, $10 an hour profit, which I thought was very fair. It was more than I had made when I was working at the office part time, so my husband said, "Continue," and I started advertising for $12 in a doll collector's directory that circulated not only in the continental United States but also in Canada and Hawaii. I began getting responses from all over, and by now I think I've gotten an order from just about every state in the Union. One of my customers from Honolulu makes ceramic dolls and competes them and has placed a very large order. As it turns out, in the same competitions several people compete dolls for which I've designed costumes.

I try to use old fabric and old trim so that the costumes look like they're old, but fraud can become a problem with this. Because I am proud of my work, I always put my label in my costumes, and I always sign them with an ink pen on the side seams to let the people know that they are indeed a new costume. There are some people who are removing the labels—not only mine, but from other costumes also—and are selling them as antique, and of course the value then can go up.

A person I know said that she saw one of my items that was being sold as an antique. I contacted the lady and dropped her business. She was sorry I felt that way. She thought it was as good as old and that's all she needed.

I've never yet had an order returned, and I suppose by now I've done more than 200 costumes. I always insure them, and I always have a return receipt so that a person can't say, "Sorry, I never received my mail."

Most all of the costumes that I do are pre-1920 back to 1860, and most of the antique dolls are from one of two countries. A lot of the older china and bisque dolls are from Germany and from France, so I do young German styles and child French dolls which at that time were very fancy.

I've done a very dark green velvet costume with mink as trim for a lady who had a 1920 bisque doll. She had all the little tails and things that she wanted me to use, so I recycled them for the doll costume, but for the most part mink wasn't used before 1920 on costumes. They used a fox drape if they used anything.

I make antique handbags, parasols, and high-button leather boots or footwear for the dolls as accessories.

My mother is very excited about the fact that I have expanded from what just started out to be a common sewing interest between us.

Contact: Karen Davies, Antique Doll Costumes, 2214 216th Street, S.E., Issaquah, Washington 98027.

Cheryl Gudinskas

CRAFT KIT DESIGNER AND WHOLESALER AND
MAIL ORDER BUSINESS OWNER,
Hawthorn Woods, Illinois.

*The women we interviewed who engaged in home mail order
businesses found mail order to be interesting and fulfilling — especially when people ordered books they had self-published or products
they had designed, manufactured, or chosen to sell. Pinpointing the
appropriate market was crucial, since sales depended largely on the
ability to reach the market through promotion — direct mail campaigns or ads in newspapers and magazines.*

Before starting this company, I was an ad manager for publishers.
Then, for about two years, I had my own free-lance commercial art
business. When the baby came, I tried to keep going with the free-
lance business and found I just couldn't do it. That kind of a business
is all deadlines, and with a new baby, I found I couldn't be
somewhere at exactly 3:00 in the afternoon, and I couldn't take the
baby around with me to my appointments. I tried, but it just wasn't
working out. You have to concentrate on the artwork, which was impossible with a new baby, so I stopped.

I lasted at home about three weeks until I started going crazy and bought a fabric craft kit to do in my spare time. I sat down with my project, and I thought it was pretty poorly designed. I called the bank at once, and asked for a loan, and that's how I started a kit business.

I had used that bank before because I'd always had to float money in and out with my free-lance commercial art business. I would buy printing, and I always needed a lot of money up front.

I borrowed $27,000. I was aware of catalog cost; I was familiar with advertising and I understood printing. I do my own designing and I save *all* the money on doing my own production on the catalog as well as on some of the photography. Despite all this knowledge and the carefully devised budget I developed, I squandered all the money on advertising the first year. Now that I've been in it for three years, I realize that I could have done everything much more efficiently. I'm starting to pay on that note, and I kick myself every time I make a payment.

My first catalog was 66 pages, and running 30,000 of them cost about $7,000 to $8,000. That was much too expensive.

As a free lance, I used to charge quite a bit for my art services. I was used to turning out quality work for slick, expensive ads and printing jobs. Now that I'm paying the bills, I intend to go into a coated newsprint-type paper instead of a more expensive paper. My customers aren't influenced by the paper quality of my catalog to buy more or less of my products, although my products would sell well only in color, and I spend too much money on good color reproduction to print the catalog on non-enamel paper. Many of my competitors, the big mail order firms, run on real light paper stock. Right now cutting down the cost of each catalog is important to me so that I can mail to more people. With the last catalog, I was in a hurry, and so I contacted a printer I knew and I said, "Do it." That's what I mean about squandering money.

Also, the very first ad I ran was a full-page full-color ad. It was not well thought out. I was so used to placing full-page ads for other people, I wasn't thinking. And this was a $7,000 ad, so, together with my first catalog run, I had spent $15,000 of that original $27,000.

I lost my shirt on that ad. The woman's magazine I placed it in had a 1,500,000 circulation, and I sold several hundred dollars' worth of products, but even so, I should have sold at least $14,000 worth of products out of it. I think one of the most valuable things I've learned in these five years is a formula. Since I know what percentage of response I'm going to get out of an ad, and I know the average sale, now I can work backward. What is the breakeven point? It boils down to how much money I can spend. I know that postage is a fixed cost. I figure that on most of these ads I can generate $5,000 or $6,000 from people ordering the catalog, since I charge $1 for the catalog. The next question is, What percentage of those people are going to buy? How much are they going to spend? I come up with a dollar figure that I'm going to gross out of that ad. Then I figure how much money I can put into the ad. What can I spend so that I don't lose money on the ad and the catalogs?

I have developed ads in which I make a free offer. If people send a dollar for the catalog, they get a free sample kit for making five gift tags. This has been very successful. Very successful means 0.5% of the total circulation, and that is very high.

I have a friend who wants to start a mail order business. She said, "I know that anyone who sees my product is going to buy two of them." This is how you start getting into trouble. A lot of people don't believe that 2% in mail order is very good. They can't believe that 100 people could look at your products and only two are going to buy. You think, "What's wrong with my product?" At least I knew that much about mail order. It would be disastrous for anyone to go in thinking they're going to sell to half of the people who saw their ad.

I have never just bought a mailing list and mailed out my catalog blindly. The cost is prohibitive. There's no way that I would ever get my money back on that. But I have gone into package-insert programs.

Most mail order companies, when shipping out their orders, insert various circulars advertising products from noncompetitive companies. I'm starting to do that as well. When I ship out orders, other companies pay me $30 a thousand to put their insert in with my packages. The very least you can spend for promotional postage is nine cents apiece bulk mail. That would cost you $90 a thousand. If you can reduce that by 30% for each insert, that's a big saving. Also, your response with the package-insert program is much higher than a blind mailing, because if you're cooperating with the right company, you're sending to people who have already bought some kind of kit, or to people who are interested in your type of product. A promotion piece first has to be approved by the company doing the shipping. If I take somebody's inserts into my package, I don't want anything competitive, or anything schlocky. I don't want anything that's going to distract from my products. There are endless possibilities for this type of promotion. For example, I'm going to contact a diaper company. There is always some sort of advertising in their weekly deliveries. I know of another company which does basically the same type of thing that I do. She was selling a stuffed hen, and she made a deal with an egg farm to put a little promotional piece inside the egg boxes so when people bought the eggs from their grocery store, and lifted up the lid, there was a little piece of paper selling her hen.

A publicity release is also good free advertising. Almost every publication has something called What's Happening or New Products. You send in a little blurb telling how much a product sells for, just as you would a catalog description, along with a black-and-white photograph. The photograph has to be able to be reduced and still be recognizable. You put "For Immediate Release" at the top, making it look somewhat professional, and maybe make a follow-up phone call. Nine times out of ten you will get your piece published. I sold a $29.95 product with a two-inch black-and-white photograph. I made hundreds of dollars out of something that cost me nothing other than the black-and-white photograph I sent to them.

You send your release to all the newspapers in the country, to the Home Living Editor, or whoever the editor is of that section of the paper. In my case, it's to the editor of every needlework magazine. I've sent press releases only a couple of times and I've had them published each time. I should just take a month off and do a whole publicity program similar to what I did for other companies when I worked for them. Every month I'd be hitting these editors with a different product. I haven't done it more often just because I haven't had the time. You could almost operate on that alone, except some of the magazines may cut you off for a while unless you start placing some advertising with them. It's important to always send good photographs because people look at the photograph first. If they're interested, they'll read on.

I worked very hard putting together my first line of products. I think I had 25 products for the first catalog. I was able to spend a great deal of time designing the products because the baby was young, and I could work through the night. She was sleeping and everything was great. I look back now at my catalog and I laugh, because I had a very strange grouping of products and I thought that everything was going to sell so well. I weeded out the "losers" with the next catalog. The biggest thing that I noticed was that people wanted to make things to give away, they don't want to make things for themselves. I had made a lot of mistakes in my judgment as to the type of products that would sell. I tend to design too much of what I would like. The things I thought were very chic for adults didn't go. I was upset because I thought I had some very contemporary designs in there, and those were not the ones that were selling. The best seller in the current catalog is the bed caddy, which doesn't have a contemporary feel at all.

There have been many surprises. For example, a very small percentage of my mail orders come from Chicago or Los Angeles or New York. They're mostly from small towns I hadn't heard of. I don't have a profile on my customers yet, but I'm working on a way of doing some kind of questionnaire without prying. I'd like to find out exactly who they are and what their interests are. I can only assume that they're basically the same people who are reading these crafts magazines: a median age of 38 and a mother with children at home.

As new product ideas pop into my head, I jot them down. When I'm ready to work on a new product, I go through the list and think of which one I want to do next. Having a child has helped. I find myself in a lot of toy stores, and by just browsing around I get an idea and say, "Hey, I could have done that better." Or being at other children's houses and seeing homemade things gives me ideas.

I knew nothing about this business before I started, so everything was new to me. The first thing that I acquired was the Commercial/Industrial Yellow Pages. I started looking under "Thread" and "Notions" and started calling around. My accountant applied for a resale number form. When I go into a store or a jobber, I just give them my resale number. This was something I had to learn about. There are many middlemen in the fabric industry.

I went to Marshall Field's (a large Chicago chain department store) where I saw the cloth that I wanted for a puppet washcloth kit. I noticed that the cloths said "Fieldcrest" on them. I looked in the Yellow Pages and found the Fieldcrest Mills and called them. They sent me to the Merchandise Mart. There I found a jobber that carried Fieldcrest, where I paid 17% higher than the mill price. Dress manufacturers might buy 500 or more yards of one material, so they can go right to the mill. The jobber is the one who has it broken up into bolts.

As the company grew, my husband quit his job for about three months to join the company and enlarge our wholesale area. On his first day he picked up a large mail order account. Then he started waking up at noon and got me in a little deeper than I wanted to be in wholesaling. I said, "Fine. We'll go into the wholesaling business, but you'd better not go back to work and dump it on me," which he said he wouldn't do but which he actually did three months later.

Wholesaling involves a lot of shopping around for prices, having thousands of kits produced, going out on a limb a lot of times. One company said they'd give me an order, but I had to be ready with an additional 500 if they needed them right away. I had to go out on a limb for that inventory, and since it's an exclusive design with them, I could never sell it to anyone else. So there's a lot of risk in volume selling. One advantage of wholesaling is that I don't have the high promotion costs. When one of my accounts wants to see my new products, I send them a photograph, and that's the extent of my costs. I don't even have the products made up as kits. If they want them, they give me enough time to make them. I love mail order. There's lots of freedom to it. Wholesaling doesn't give me that freedom. I'm always at the beck and call of my accounts, and I don't like that, but it means more money, which I need to develop the mail order end of the business.

For a very short time, we did sell to retail shops, but it's harder to make money that way. First of all, you have to give them at least 50% off. Stores will order two here, five there. Now if you go to *Better Homes and Gardens* or The Stitchery, they have 5,000,000 on their lists, and they'll give you a good order up front.

I fluctuate back and forth on my business objectives. In the beginning, it was for money alone, and then I thought, "No, no. It really doesn't make that much difference." Well, now it's starting to make a difference again. The enthusiasm for having my own thing is waning, and now I don't want to keep working this hard unless I'm going to start showing a big profit on it. I see that it's possible, and the accountant says, "You have a solid foundation here, and if you keep going, you'll make it, but it will be slow." It's probably going to take another three years. I showed my first profit this year, so I'm on my way.

These past three years have been a lot of fun for me. I suppose I also realize that I'm stuck with it. I have this business loan, and I can't afford to start thinking that it isn't fun. I enjoy going to the post office, and each time someone orders something that I've designed, I get this little ego trip. I designed some murals for myself and don't even have them hanging in the house. I was too sensitive to criticism and to people analyzing things in front of me. When an order comes in, it's a positive comment on my achievements.

For catalogue send $1.00 to: Cher's Kit and Kaboodle, P.O. Box 71, Vernon Hills, Illinois 60061.

Freude Bartlett

FILM DISTRIBUTOR AND PRODUCER,
Oakland, California.

About one-third of the women we interviewed attributed the success-ful marketing of their product or service to being in the right place at the right time and then being able to take advantage of the situation. Freude Bartlett had flown to New York without a plan for distributing her husband's film. She only knew that New York was the place to go for his type of film. And it so happened that she was in New York when the annual American Film Festival was being held.

There were 15-minute breaks between screenings. I asked to use a projector during breaks, and by going into the hallways and literally grabbing librarians by the arm, I managed to fill up the room in which I showed my husband's film. . . . Sure enough, I sold a lot of prints.

I could say, I began in film distribution by falling in love with a film-maker, but easy as that explanation is, it is only partially true. The truth is always long and complicated. When I was 18 and a philoso-phy student in New York, I passed a storefront where "underground" movies were being shown. I went in, and the film I saw, *A Movie*, by Bruce Conner, opened my eyes to the possibility of film as an art form. Its potential seemed much greater than the narrative uses I'd become accustomed to in Hollywood movies. I saw that an artist could use film to make art just as a painter uses oil and watercolor.

It wasn't until I returned to California four years later, with no money, my young daughter Samantha, and an uncertain future that I decided to go to film school at San Francisco State. I studied film, worked as the Film Department secretary, and was art editor of the school film magazine. After two years of film school, I met my second husband. He made a spectacular experimental film, and at the time neither of us knew anything about the film distribution business, but I figured that I had 5,000 years of mercantile, middle-class Jewish blood in me and that I could learn how — and I did.

After our honeymoon, I flew to New York and started with the Museum of Modern Art, where I showed the film and asked, "What should I do? Who will buy this film? It's great art." The curator responded, "Yes, it's wonderful, but you're going to have trouble finding anyone to buy it. The first place you should go is across the street to the Donnell Branch of the New York Public Library."

I ran across the street, and when I asked for the film librarian, his colleague told me, "He's not here and he won't be back for a week." I said, "Oh, my God, I'm only going to be here a week. Where is he?" It turned out that he was at the Hilton Hotel, where the American Film Festival was being held, so I walked to the Hilton and took the escalator upstairs to the festival. It was like landing in Paradise. Most public libraries buy films in the same way they buy books, and there were 2,000 film librarians from all over the country milling about at the festival. All the important film distributors were exhibiting their newest films. They had booths and suites where films that were in the competition were being screened. There were 15-minute breaks between screenings. I asked to use a projector during breaks, and by going into the hallways and literally grabbing librarians by the arm, I managed to fill up the room in which I showed my husband's film. I had no idea what the film should sell for, but in checking someone's catalogue I discovered that a similar-length work was priced at $350. Sure enough, I sold a lot of prints. It had not occurred to me for a moment that I wasn't going to succeed.

For several years I acted as my husband's distributor, manager, business agent, producer, cook, and housekeeper. During that time I had my second child, Adam, while my husband continued to make films which made money. We reinvested the money in film equipment and more filmmaking. But there was not then, and there isn't now, a big market for the kind of experimental work he was doing. From the beginning, I had written articles for magazines about film as an art form and spoken to community groups, seminars, classes, etc. I've always been concerned with establishing a climate for the acceptance and appreciation of this kind of work.

And so it was that I learned the mechanics of distribution. All during this time I had been making films myself though not distributing them, since I concentrated on distributing my husband's work. Enter the Women's Movement! I joined a consciousness-raising group made up of other artists and other artists' wives. At the same time I started showing my work publicly and began to realize and enjoy the ability I had as a filmmaker to communicate to large audiences. Still, I found myself talking about the same frustrations week after week in my group. Finally I stepped back and took a look at the fact that nothing would change for me unless *I* changed first, and for me the first step meant dissolving my marriage.

When I got divorced in the early 1970s, I was 29, with $1,000 in the bank, and a skill which had been applied only to managing the financial interests of a single filmmaker. There was no reason not to get serious — thus Serious Business Company. All along a lot of filmmakers had asked me to distribute their work. Now I called them back and agreed to do so.

I put together a film catalogue and printed 2,000 copies at a cost of exactly $1,000. It wasn't until I was driving back from the printer that I realized I didn't have another cent. I didn't have the money to pay the rent and I didn't have the money to mail out the catalogue! A couple of days later, a taxi cab ran into my car. The $700 I collected from the insurance company paid the rent and the postage on the mailing.

Film distribution is a mail order business by and large. Doing a healthy business is based on distributing one's catalogue to the greatest number of potential users as well as on carefully placed advertising and attending film conferences and seminars. Obviously, having a first-rate product comes before all else. Serious Business Company concentrates on films that appeal to me for their artistic and/or educational merits. I take unusual and innovative works. We represent a wide range of films, including avant-garde works: anima-tion, short narratives, and social and anthropological documentaries. We sell to both theatrical and nontheatrical markets, with an emphasis on libraries, universities, community groups, movie theaters, and worldwide television.

In 1973 when my own film *Women and Children* was reviewed by *Ms.* magazine and I received many orders for it, I realized there was a largely untapped market for films by and about women. Since then I've made a point of including films with a feminist point of view, and I've made a particular effort to acquaint women's organizations with their availability.

In 1977 I published 20,000 copies of a 160-page catalogue with more than 200 films represented. From that mailing I doubled my gross. Now, however, with Proposition 13 causing tighter budgets in California and inflation hitting nationwide, film distribution is especial-ly difficult. We've expanded in certain areas and cut back in others. Recently we've begun distributing packages of animated shorts to film repertory houses that show classics and to theaters that specialize in art films. We also distribute shorts to be played with feature films. For instance, Sally Cruikshank's animated film *Make Me Psychic* played with *The China Syndrome* for more than four months.

Eventually there won't be any more 16-mm film distribution. Everything will be on video. You'll be able to buy a full-length feature on a cassette or video disk for the price of a record album. We already offer every title in our catalogue on video cassette.

In the past eight years I don't think I've become any less idealistic, but I have become more realistic about what kinds of policies are necessary to keep a small business afloat and leave it room to grow. I began knowing absolutely nothing and learned as I went along. I was carried along by ideology and the emotional satisfaction my success gave me. A large part of nurturing any business is devloping relation-ships with people. It isn't so different from raising children or making movies.

There is a lot of creative intelligence involved in business, but it is not the same thing as material creativity, making something original from scratch. I miss enormously producing something that is uniquely and completely my own. Aside from the business, a great deal of my energy goes to my children.

I don't have much room for waking dream time, but still the urge comes along when everything is quiet, when the phones stop ringing, and everyone has gone home. It surfaces in the form of ideas, images, and visions. Even though I have vowed to get back to more creative work, I don't regret having spent all this time on business. I want a life that accommodates both impulses.

For catalogue write: Serious Business Company, 1145 Mandana Boulevard, Oakland, California 94610.

Arlene Winkler

PRODUCTION WEAVER,
Newton, Massachusetts.

After finding that their products were not selling well, two of the craftswomen we interviewed told how they had meticulously assessed the problem and redesigned their line of crafts until they began to make a profit. In Arlene Winkler's case, it meant changing from pillows, wall hangings, and little vests to specializing in clothing for men and women.

I was doing things that were being done, and there were a whole lot of people who did it better than I. Who needed me? But that's what paying your dues is all about.

Her weaving line became well recognized and established in some of the best Boston and New York department store designer showrooms. She has had one-woman shows and participated as a production weaver in the prestigious Rhinebeck, New York, Craft Fair. Her work has also been exhibited in a men's woven clothing show at the Smithsonian Institution.

When I was 9 years old, my mother taught me to sew. By the time I was 16, she had taught me to draft patterns. She, by the way, was practically self-taught. Her grandfather was a tailor, and although she was a musically gifted person, there was some kind of emotional safety in sewing.

Foolishly I married at 19. I tried all kinds of things to keep myself happy. I discovered that I was most self-satisfied when I could do something that brought in some kind of money. I did free-lance costuming for advertising agencies. If anybody needed something special made — decorators, ad agencies, etc. — I would figure out a way to make it. The problem solving intrigued me. Technically I could find people who could do it better than I, if needed, and that was another problem to solve. But the *how* of it — how to go about it, how to find things, how to find the people to do it, how to work out the small pieces of the problems, the construction — that was the part that I liked.

Although when I remarried, I married a man 10 years younger than I was, Bob was also a problem solver, and so we had a great deal in common. He bought me a loom for my birthday. I had never woven, but I had always been interested. I began to look for weaving classes when I realized how little I knew.

I heard about an apprenticeship, and that was more interesting to me. I became an apprentice to Lillian Ball, who was 19 at the time, and I was 35. When I began the apprenticeship, my third child was only nine months old, and the problem of how to balance my life began immediately. I stayed with Lillian a year and a half and then went into business.

I didn't have any start-up capital. My husband loaned me money, which I paid back into the household out of my sales. First he loaned me babysitting money so that I could do the apprenticeship, and then he loaned me money to buy materials. It was very tight all along. It was very, very hard. He wasn't making that much money, and it was difficult, but Bob gave me encouragement to go forward with my craft, to move into business and to be professional. I felt that I was a person in business then, and I wasn't conflicted as I was the first time around. I had created the failure in the other businesses that I had attempted during my first marriage. I was conflicted then because I felt that my house wasn't clean enough and I felt that I should be sewing dresses for my daughter instead of trying to sew a line of children's clothes. I don't think that I've ever made mistakes in this current business as a result of feeling guilty about what I "should" be doing.

I began doing craft shows to bring my product to market and get a response — or lack of response, as it turned out. I did a Christmas show and I bombed! I made about $60, and I was there four or five days. There were days in that show where I was so depressed I wanted to leave. I finally decided that even if I didn't sell another thing, it would be a personal triumph to stay at the damn show and just *be there*, and smile at people as they walked past my merchandise.

One thing that kept me going when things were down was that I was really jealous of Lillian. She had created something that people wanted. I had done shows with her and I had seen people respond to her product, and I wanted people to respond to my things the same way. I wanted people to look at my things and say, "It's too expensive. I can't afford it, but I have to have it." Another thing was the feeling that I *could* come up with it, that I knew a lot, and that I could bring all the things I had done all my life together and do something successful. My husband remained tremendously supportive.

I decided that I would do only clothing. It was very clear that people would put money on their backs. People love to buy clothing. I began to work in sensually appealing fibers, in silks, in chenille, in cotton. The things I made were designed to go on your naked body and feel fabulous! Furthermore, everything was softly fitted so it was comfortable to wear. These were all the things that I insisted on when I looked for clothing. It should feel good on my skin. It should fit comfortably. It should look like clothing, but it shouldn't look like anything else that you could possibly buy in a store or factory made.

I wanted my designs to look good on men, too. Why should I limit my market? I made my clothing in small, medium, and large for men and small, medium, and large for women, and the shapes were loom shapes, basically "T." The neckline was woven and there was no shoulder seam. The sleeves were sewed on. Each thing was plotted so that I could take everything off one warp. I didn't have to do a sleeve warp and then a body warp.

I think the first year that I was in business was really important because that was when I created my product, that was when my look was created, that was when I began to choose fibers and to become expert in the thing that I did. That was kind of an apprenticeship to myself.

Again I did the Christmas show. I got an enormous response to my things. I was so encouraged. I brought $2,000 worth of things with me for that Christmas show, and I sold almost everything. I had brought a lot of men's things — shirts and full-length caftans. At all the shows I noticed that it was the men who came in and handled stuff and commented on the good-feeling things. I kept saying to myself, "That's your market, Arlene." These people don't ask me, "How much does it cost?" when they buy. They say, "I'll take that. Wrap it up," and then, "How much is it?" The fact that the stuff felt good appealed to women, too. At a show I just did, a woman bought a full-length caftan. She put it on and she kept saying, "Ooh, it's so friendly."

I knew that my production line was safe. I knew it sold well, and I knew the variations I could do on it, but it wasn't enough for my own self-fulfillment. I needed to do risky pieces. It was important to me to take a risk and to know I was going to learn from it.

After the Christmas show, I had a one-woman show, and I got the attention of another craftswoman who uses a representative. She called me and said, "I'd like to show your things to my rep." The rep turned out to be a 27-year-old woman from a fabulously wealthy family who shops in stores that carry designers' things. Up to that point, I hadn't done any wholesaling. I had gone to New York and attempted to sell my things, and I had not succeeded. This woman only wanted 10%. What does it cost me to lose time from the business, to get on a plane, to go to a city and eat my meals out? What did I have to lose? She turned out to be very, very good. She was at her ease in those stores that really make me uptight. She knew the buyers, and she did quite well for me.

When I started, I had one line in dark strong colors and that was it. The next thing I knew, somebody called me who had seen me at the show and said, "Can we see your spring line?" I said, "Sure. It's not off the looms yet." Then I realized that if I'm going to play this game, I'd better find out the rules. Now I have a summer line and I have a winter line. The summer line also gets sold for cruise wear.

The profit rate for this business is about 19%, which is not a very big rate of profit at all. Possibly I could get it up to 25%, but that's about it. I'd like to get volume up enough so that the dollars will come in. There's no way that I can draw enough money out of the household any more to increase the business. If the reps bring in the orders and I can show my good business history to a bank, I'll go for a loan. I'll take on more weavers and more stitchers and really get going.

The other part of my goal is to get myself out of the production end of it and be the person who does the designing, solves production problems, runs the business, and has a little time left over, which, at this point, I don't.

The craft end of it is full of amateurs who are idealistic people who want to make a well-made product but don't want to charge enough for their merchandise, and that really burns me. I'm tired of being undercut by people who do beautiful work and are selling it for less than I do. I know what it costs me to produce something. I know how much I *must* make on an item, and that's how I set my prices.

The business will either grow enormously or I'll fold it and concentrate on doing one-of-a-kind pieces. I can't see changing the nature of the products very much. I treasure growth along with fun, and that means change.

I like the designing most and getting feedback for the designs. When I was a housewife, nobody ever told me, "Boy, you sure scrub that toilet beautifully." I like to have people say to me, "This is just beautiful. I'm glad I bought it. I want to wear it a lot." That really makes me feel good. It makes me feel like I'm spending my time well, and that's important. The older I get, the more I realize how short life is.

A year and a half later Arlene told us:

I've closed down my business. Three things happened that influenced my decision. The first was that a mail order craft business, which accounted for $10,000 of my $20,000 gross a year, went bankrupt, owing me several thousand dollars. All the way along I was fighting undercapitalization, and that was just the last straw. The second reason was my growing discouragement, and my feeling that I was chained to the loom. I hadn't succeeded in getting more involved in the designing and promoting aspects of the business. The third reason was that my husband made me a very good offer to come into his graphic design business as an account representative. Although I don't get that continuous ego stroking that I got from my own business when people reacted to my designs, I am again able to take all that I learned about promotion and other business skills and put it to use in new ways.

I think life is a series of phases, and my production business was one of the important phases in my life. What I learned then is serving me beautifully in this new phase, while at the same time I'm experiencing the stimulation of new growth.

Chris Birchfield

MANUFACTURER OF CANVAS BAGS
AND MAIL ORDER BUSINESS OWNER,
Cornish, Maine.

*Over and over, women told us that quality of their product or service
was a basic concern. They also treated their employees with great
respect, not only by paying them as much as they possibly could, but
also by expressing their appreciation. Chris Birchfield is representative of the women we talked with throughout the country who
demonstrated a self-imposed high standard of employee treatment.*

Our women work on the premise that the person who ends up
with this bag must feel that that's the only bag we ever made. I don't
have one woman sitting at a machine putting on all pockets and one
woman putting on all the straps and another woman sewing up the
edges. We don't work like that because they won't take pride in what
they're doing then. Now obviously when you're doing 10,000 bags a
year, sometimes quality slips a little, but nothing goes out of here that *I*
don't see. I do all the ribbons and all the silk-screening, so obviously I
control that end of it. I have very good people working for me and I
pay a premium price. I don't have a woman who earns under $4.80
(1978) an hour ever. That's good money for Cornish women. Most
places around here, like the dress factory, pay minimum wage. There

are quite a few sewing operations in the area, and a lot of the women run piece work, but they don't usually average much over $3 or $3.50 even if they're really fast. I can't say that I've made lots of money. Most weeks they make more than I do, but I have the freedom that I might not have if I had to get dressed up and go to town to work.

I started in March 1976 because I needed money and I wanted to get out of a bad job situation. We'd been married for only three years and Dave, my second husband, had been laid off from his job. We were on this farm, and we'd been there for only six months when it happened.

The only job I could get — it didn't make any difference that I had any kind of education at all — was driving a school bus. It was a horrible job.

If you grew up with something and then you become poor, it's just the worst feeling. The only good thing about it is that you have hope that things will improve, but when you don't have two dimes in your pocket or you can't call the garage to come fix the car because you don't have the money, it's a desperate situation.

Well, L. L. Bean, the 24-hour-a-day hunting and clothing outfitter, which is sort of a Maine institution, sold a canvas bag that was white on top and either navy blue or red on the bottom. It was ugly as sin and it wasn't very well made. I said, "I can do better than that!"

I happened to pick up an issue of *Woman's Day* that showed how to make canvas seat covers, and it gave some places to buy canvas wholesale. I was just so tickled because I knew that that was what I needed to get started.

I took my last paycheck, I quit the bus driving job, and I rented a building uptown here in Cornish. I couldn't work on the farm because we had no electricity. I took my $17 worth of canvas and my little home machine and I went up there in this great big building 60′×20′ and I started producing canvas bags. Obviously $17 didn't go very far, but I had a big window and I put all my stock of six or seven bags in the window. Someone came in, because of course, being in a small town, they're always interested in what's going on in town, and bought one. I think I sold the first bag for $6 or $7, which already was practically half of my initial investment with the exception of the rent.

I told Dave that we'd give it six months and if I couldn't meet the rent payments then we would call it a draw and I'd go back and find something else to do. And it worked. We managed to meet the rent payments. A real skin-of-your-teeth operation.

The landlord went from $100 a month on the rent to $120 to $150 and, in a year and a half's time, was telling me I had a $200-a-month rent to pay. I said, "With a house mortgage, too, this is insane to pay $200 a month to run some sewing machines."

About the same time I was getting very upset over the farm. It was just not the idyllic place that it might have been if we'd had the money and the time to put into it. It was getting to be a very bad situation for me. I just couldn't take the back-to-nature thing. I wasn't brought up that way and I had a very hard time adjusting to it.

It never had any bathroom. It never had any electricity. It never had any plumbing. We had never done anything like that before. We dug a well. We put in new sills. We did everything! Well, when you work 12 hours a day and you're running a business, there isn't much time left for that. We ended up being pretty nasty to each other. I said the only way to save our marriage as far as I was concerned was to get out of that house. It was really destroying us. David set up a certain criterion. If I could find a house in a certain price range that we could move the business into, and we could sell the farm in the same amount of time so that the transfer was easy, he'd go for it.

My little fanny went out trotting up and down Cornish, looking. I knew this house had been on the market and I was always fascinated by it. I thought to myself, Hey, I'll bet we could work in that barn upstairs, and downstairs, someday, maybe we could put a shop.

We put the farm on the market and it sold for cash so that they didn't have to go through the bank, and it was an ideal situation. I'm a great believer in the Lord God who takes care of us if we take care of ourselves. He . . . She arranged that for me.

Sometimes I think about it and I don't know *how* I did it. We bought our sixth commercial machine the other day. I have taken two loans out in my business career, to establish a good credit rating for me as a woman, as well as to rehabilitate my credit rating when Dave was out of work and we had some real financial problems.

Now we owe nobody anything. Everything that comes in the door pays the bills right off. That's been hard at times, when you have six people on the payroll and Friday afternoon rolls around. That's anywhere from $600 to $800 a week worth of payroll to meet, and that's a big amount of money for our size business to put out. We just hired the sixth person. We got to a point where we couldn't get things out within 21 days, and that was the time to put somebody else on to relieve the strain.

A year and a half ago, after the business was really going, a man came in the door before Christmas and he said, "I'd like to represent you." I didn't know what he was talking about. I said, "I can't talk to you now. I'm really busy. It's before Christmas, and this isn't the time to talk business. Come on back." He said, "Well, I'll give you my card." I threw it on the desk and I thought afterwards, I was really rude to him. He may be a good deal for me, dummy! But somebody else was here at the time, and I was giving them my attention.

He had seen my bags at a store. I called Cindy, the woman who owns the store, and we talked about it. I felt that if she had confidence in him then he must be all right. He represented other good firms. He came back in February, and I still have him with us. He covers all of Maine and New Hampshire for us.

I've taken on two more reps during the year to do other parts of the country. Our prices have been a little under the rest of the wholesalers because we felt it would get us in the door, but it's time now to up them, and I don't feel badly about it. I feel it's a necessity.

I always had the feeling that if we made a bag just a little bit better and charged the same price as the guy down the street, then in time we could charge a good price for ours and yet put a better bag on the market. I've had buyers come back who've gone to the shows in New York and said to me, "You know, we just couldn't find a better bag. We're buying again from you."

We were contacted by the wholesale market in Bedford, Massachusetts, which is a great big enormous permanent showroom marketplace. I have not been particularly pleased, with the exception of one very good account we landed through them in Boston. It's a tiny shop called The Irresistibles. They do nothing but canvas bags, and now 90% of the bags they carry are ours. They're really pleased with the quality and the look. Cindy calls on Sunday nights usually and says, "I need four dozen of this and four dozen of that." We're very good about getting her order out in a week. Now she has two stores, another in Marblehead she's just opened. The personal touch is there with people like that. And that's the kind of $1,000-a-month account that I don't want to lose, so we maintain it very closely, but the 15% fee paid to the showroom in Bedford hurts. It's the only good account we've gotten from them. I thought we would get into department stores through them.

When the order comes in the door I look at it first, and then I make a list of the colors that I want, for that particular store. Then I give it to the cutter. Even though I haven't been to most of the stores we wholesale to, I know what their line is, so I work out their colors.

Businesswise my priority is to enable my husband to not have to go to Portland to work, not to give him his freedom, because you can't give anybody their freedom really, but to enable him to have as much fun as I'm having. As far as I'm concerned, I've really got the world by the tail in this situation. I'd like to see me as the director, with the *baton*, orchestrating it, and really making it a dynamic, successful thing.

Early in 1980 Chris wrote:

Things are absolutely booming here — 29 on the payroll and doing business at a rate of half a million dollars a year. I'm in the process of filling a $100,000 order for a chain store. As for directing with baton—well, that's about right. It's extremely hectic but financially and mentally worth it.

For catalogue write: Accessories Unlimited of Maine, Main Street, Cornish, Maine 04020.

Sue Crawford and Carol Royko

DESIGNERS AND MANUFACTURERS OF GREETING CARDS,
Chicago, Illinois.

Again and again we found that women home business owners are compassionately sensitive to the needs of others — senior citizens, children, those who need special help. Sue and Carol started their business because of the way dying people are treated. Their dedication to developing a line of supportive greeting cards led them to interview terminally ill patients to find out what words and thoughts brought them comfort.

Sue: We started this business two years ago because there was a need. I had friends who were dying of cancer, and Carol's parents have been ill for a long time in a nursing home, so we were sensitized to the needs of the dying. People would constantly ask me as a writer and poet, "What should I say to people with cancer?" One day Carol set up a darkroom, and I said, "We are going into business." That's how we began. Carol is a photographer; she sees things and I hear things and we put our talents together to make our "I Care" collection of greeting cards.

We wanted to test our ideas on cancer patients to make sure our cards made them feel good. To begin with, we took our photographs and verses to a 50-year-old woman who was dying of cancer, and she said, "I hate cats, hate dogs, hate this, hate that, I don't like pictures, I don't like that verse, hate children, that one's depressing," but she thought it was a very good idea, and she said we should go to somebody else and get other opinions. So she wasn't only negative.

I have enough Scotch in me that I said, "We're not going to give up!" Carol felt the same way and she talked to Art Schneider, who was the science writer for the *Daily News* at that time.

Carol: He was very, very happy that someone was going to develop such a card line, and he helped us a lot. He told us where to go to talk to people who ran the Make the Day Count groups, which are self-help group-therapy-type organizations for cancer outpatients. Through them, we got in touch with other cancer patients.

Sue: I would take my three children who were 5, 7, and 10 years old at the time along with the pictures and the words to go to visit people who couldn't leave their homes but who wanted to take the test. Many of them had heard about it and would call and say, "Come and give me the test."

We numbered each line and each photograph, and the patients would write their comments for each one. We tested not only the patients but also their families and people who worked with patients.

It was hard to talk to deformed people about dying, but we knew in our hearts that it was something that had to be done, because people need to face up to the fact that dying people want to be recognized as human beings with feelings, not as dying Things. The patients would show us cards that they had received. One card said, "Get up off of your ass." These were sent to people who were terribly ill, and the messages hurt them.

Through the testing we found that words that *we* liked often turned the patients off. Things that we thought were beautiful made them angry, because certain words and thoughts like "I need you" meant demands to them. They didn't want to know how the sender felt. They would say, "Don't say that. Don't command me to do anything."

We knew that although our cards worked for patients with terminal illnesses, they also worked for others. A friend who was in a hospital for a long time with a nervous breakdown got hideous cards that made her feel awful — but our cards made her feel good. I decided to test other mental patients and see how they felt about our cards. They loved them. The words and thoughts were meaningful to them. "Courage." "Patience." "Take my hand so I can walk with you." I understand where you're at." And we did understand where they were at.

Carol: We found that our cards applied to anyone with any life-threatening disease or in any trauma.

Sue: A woman that I know just recently got a divorce and is going through a lot of hassle. I sent her a card with one word, "Patience." She loved it. She said it was wonderful because "I want everything over today. I want it done."

Carol: Our cards can also be used to express sympathy. Most sympathy cards today are just horrible. I had a friend whose 17-year-old son was killed in an automobile accident. God, what do you say? I sent her "Friends are for loving and sharing everything." And then I just wrote at the bottom, "We share your grief."

My mother has had multiple sclerosis for 15 years and is paralyzed from the waist down. She's got a cancerous tumor on the kidney that she's refused surgery for. Mother's Day came, and we had cards for Dad to send to her, for us to give to her, for her grandchildren to give to her. My mother has been watching us as we developed our cards, and she had tears in her eyes because the cards were so beautiful.

Once the testing was completed and we had singled out the pictures and verses the patients liked, we had to put them together and have the pictures say what the verse meant and vice versa. Then we had to have them printed. The business end of it has been very hard because we're total novices.

Sue: We went to a bank and we got a loan. While Carol was out of town, the vice-president of the bank called me and said, "What are you putting up for collateral?"

"Our brains," I said.

"What did you say?" he asked.

"Our brains," I repeated.

He said, "I can't take that to the loan board."

"That's what you're going to have to take," I said, "because not only are we very creative people with high IQ's but we're stubborn, and if you don't give us the loan, somebody else will."

He took that to the loan board, and we got the loan, which was for $8,000.

Carol: We already owed $3,000 to the printer who printed our samples. We kept making mistakes, and the runs had to be made over again. He never gave us an itemized bill, and he kept implying that it would cost very little. When we asked how much money we owed him, he said, "$3,000."

We marketed our cards in three different ways. (1) We did a 1,000-piece direct mail campaign to hospital gift shops across the country; (2) we obtained some space at the McCormick Place Gift Show to sell to buyers from all over; and (3) in the Chicago area, we sold directly to big stores and florists, who had never before carried cards. The mailing produced 60 clients even though the U.S. Postal Service lost all the pieces that we sent to the Chicago-area hospitals.

Sue: We got eight orders during the four days we spent at the Gift Show, and one of them was from a distributor who has 40 salesmen throughout the country. People were amazed that, as a new company, we even got eight orders.

There are a million lines of cards, and unless you have something really special, Hallmark or Norcross have it better and they have the money to promote. Another problem is that as soon as you come up with a good idea and you produce it, even if you may have a copyright on that card, somebody can change one word or change the picture and it's their line. That's called knocking off! Since we have developed our card line based on what patients want, if people try to "knock us off," they're going to have to do a little thinking. They can't just change a single word because it won't work.

The big stores remove our line before Mother's Day, Christmas, Easter, and Thanksgiving because they need the space for specialty cards. How can we run a business when they take us out, particularly at those times?

Our cards retail for 75¢, and we sell them for 37½¢ to the stores. If we're lucky, we end up making a dime a card. The more we print, the cheaper it is, but then we could lose, too. If we've got 1,000 cards sitting as inventory (and we've got to pay for that inventory out of profits) how can we afford to redesign and run more when we haven't paid for the first run?

Carol: We have 24 cards at this point, but we've redone the whole line because we weren't getting reorders. Everybody who works with cards said that they were too heavy and that the sepia tone color, which the patients picked out, was wrong.

Sue: One little old lady at Marshall Field's who's been there forever and who knows cards said, "Listen to me" — and we did. She's the one executives upstairs ask, "What do you think about this card?" They really respect her opinion. She thinks these will do well.

We've also got much encouragement from the hospital gift shops. They wrote us, "Thank God someone's finally done it!"

Carol: They put the cards in the rack but don't use our leader cards which explain in a short paragraph what our cards are all about. Our cards are in the rack but people are walking past them. They're not picking them out. They can't respond because they don't know how the cards developed or the difference between our line and other card lines. We're going to look into 10- or 15-second radio commercials on major stations so that people know our cards are available.

Sue: Potential purchasers have to know the line is available. When people are deathly ill, so ill they can hardly sit up and still they take the test and say, "Get those out for us. We need them!" you better believe we're going to get these cards known! The trick is to have people recognize the name, the "I Care" collection.

After the *Sun-Times* article on our business, a neurologist told me, "What you women are doing is one of the most needed things. I deal with brain cancer. I deal with nerve disease. Your work is fabulous. Don't stop."

What hurts us most is that some of the women and men who took the test have since died. They never really got to see the cards become a success as they wanted, to become as available as Hallmark cards. But we get this feeling that they're with us.

The "I Care" collection is only one part of our business, The Artist's Notebook, Inc. We have other ideas. If we make money on this, we can go on to something else.

Sue and Carol's interview was conducted in May 1979. On September 19, 1979, Carol Royko died suddenly of a brain embolism. The business was closed down because it was too painful for Sue to continue it. Sue told us:

I feel we were successful. We showed people that there was a need for these cards. The business was a *personal* success for me, too, for through Carol and her support as a business partner, and as my closest friend, she has left me with a tremendous amount of creative energy and strength to go on. Carol made me feel I could do anything, and now I have begun work on a new and exciting idea which I feel will be worthwhile and successful.

Susan Armbrecht

TELEPHONE SOLICITOR,
Cleveland, Ohio.

Specialized equipment helps the physically disabled to perform certain types of work.

Since I am physically disabled, the equipment is adapted to me and I can dial the phone numbers myself. It's a regular push-button phone with a special set-up where I can get the dial tone without using my hand. I pay a rate for the push-button phone, but not for the special equipment. I don't really need a lot of equipment. I need my voice. That's my special equipment.

The trouble is, the work is often not equal to the person's mental capabilities, and the choice becomes working with what is available or not working at all.

I do telephone soliciting for a moving company in Cleveland. I got started about 12 years ago when another woman who was working from her home doing this type of work for the company decided she wanted to retire. It was an ideal situation for someone who was disabled.

I call people who are selling their homes to find out if they are going to be using professional movers, and I set up appointments for our various agents to go in and make an estimate on how much it would cost people to move with our company. I get paid by commission. I get a flat fee if I can get the estimator in the door, and then, if he books the lead, I get a percentage.

We specialize in long-distance moves, so when I ask, "Are you moving local or long distance?" depending on what their answer is, I handle it in one of two ways. If they say they're moving locally, then I say I'm sorry to have bothered you. If they say that they're moving long distance, I ask if they're planning to use movers. Usually they say yes, and I either try to get them to make an appointment right then or I call them back and send a brochure. Then I indicate to my company whether or not it's a referral.

During the summer I work three to four solid days on the phone. People are moving the minute the schools let out so that they can be settled by September, and I am on the phone most of the time. During the summer I get close to three hundred new listings a week. I may get only 50% of the people at home the first time I call; otherwise it's a matter of recalling and recalling.

People are generally home between seven and nine, but I call during the day as well as at night. Monday and Tuesday nights are my best nights, but I'm on the phone five hours a day both those days, too. It's very tiring. Once I've started, it's better not to stop if I'm going to accomplish anything. Besides being physically tiring, it's emotionally draining.

After working three-and-a-half to four days solid on the phone, I don't have the strength or the personality to deal with people Friday through Sunday. Each phone call is a potential client, so if I get physically tired or cannot open my mouth another minute, it does reflect on the business. I have to keep a certain pitch and maintain a certain amount of personal charm to get through.

People are very willing to listen if I make it short and get their attention real fast and don't waste their time. About 95% of the people are very agreeable, but I also get cranks and people who say, "You have no business calling me." *I* would feel resentment if someone bothered me, so I'm always polite and say, "I'm sorry I bothered you" and hang up. I really don't have much contact with people who are difficult.

Anyone could do it. It's a matter of whether they want to do it or not. It isn't exciting. It's repetitive and it tends to be very boring. I don't really feel very fulfilled or satisfied unless I can get involved in how many sales I've made that day, but after a while that sort of wears thin. It would be a good situation for someone to supplement an income, but not to sustain herself.

The only way I could improve my position would be to expand into other areas of sales, and I really don't want to do that. This consumes a lot of my time as it is now, and it doesn't leave me much personal time, except in winter, which I need in order to recharge myself for the summer.

Work to me is not the total part of my life. It's just enough to keep me going and to give me something to do. I don't find it necessarily very satisfying or fulfilling. I feel very competent in what I do, and I know I'm good, but there are other things I could do also.

I like being independent of the office. I don't have someone standing over me saying I have to make 800 phone calls this week. No one bothers me. They trust me to do the work, and I bring in enough business to warrant their trust and confidence. I work at my own rate and my own time, and I like that sense of independence. If I want to take a day off, I take a day off. I have a certain amount to do, and I get it done very well.

Mary Ellen Donald

AUTHOR,
MUSICIAN,
INSTRUCTOR,
MAIL ORDER
BUSINESS OWNER,
San Francisco,
California.

All six women we interviewed who could compensate for a physical handicap and who had initiative and determination attained self-fulfillment and/or profit through their home business. Mary Ellen Donald is legally blind, yet she not only plays the drum for Middle Eastern dancers, she has written the first English instruction manuals on Middle Eastern drums and cymbals and she distributes them through her own mail order business.

Because I'm not able to see very well, I have to do some unique things. I have asked dancers to dance right close to me, like a foot away. Although I can't see the details of what a dancer is doing, I can get a sense of whether her hips are making big movements or small movements and we can have a back-and-forth dialogue. Otherwise I have to depend on people in the band to give me verbal signals like, "Now!" or "Stop!" or "Change!"

I had just finished my graduate work in psychiatric social work, and after spending so many years doing head-work in school, I was tired. I wanted to develop more of my body and my sensuous being rather than just my intellect, so I decided to find a dance form that would allow me to do that. It was just by chance that my husband met a woman at work who was excited about belly dancing and who took me to a lesson. I loved it. I went every week and practiced two hours every day.

I have a musical background. I took piano lessons for eight years, studied voice for a year, sang in a chorus or choir all my life, and even went to Spain, where I studied flamenco guitar for a year. I was able to play the finger cymbals with such ease that my dance instructor suggested I learn the drum. She thought if she had her own musicians in her own group, then she would have an easier time putting on performances, because she wouldn't have to depend upon those few musicians in the area who played Middle Eastern drum. So I took up the drum. That was ten years ago.

Meanwhile, for three years I worked full time at Catholic Social Services doing family and individual counseling, mostly with Spanish-speaking clients. I left the agency just before our son was born, seven years ago, and I didn't want to go back to a full-time job. I wanted to stay home and take care of John, but I also wanted to keep up with my skills, so I had three clients in a private practice. As time went on, however, I felt I really didn't have the right kind of psychological framework to continue. Even though I was learning new techniques through additional training after graduate school, I decided that what I was doing was not coming from something I had experienced in my life. I was only trying out other people's notions and mouthing other people's theories, and that was not very satisfying for me.

Then came economic troubles. My husband left his job to get his master's degree, and when he went back to work for the city, he wasn't making much money. On top of that, we had used credit cards on a big trip the year before, and we were in debt. I wanted to continue my belly dance lessons, but I couldn't even pay the $4 a week to take the class, so Bert Balladine, my new dance instructor, said, "Why don't we work out some kind of an exchange?" "All right," I said, "I'll play the drums and provide live music for your class, and you let me take the lessons free." So that's what we did.

One day I was practicing the drum, and a girl who heard me asked me to teach her—and that was the beginning. A few months later, I taught drums to several others who were studying belly dancing, and then I realized it would be easier for the students if I would mimeograph the lessons so they wouldn't have to spend half their lesson copying from the blackboard. Also, since there was no manual in English on how to play Middle Eastern drums or rhythms, I decided to put together a little booklet and perhaps charge 50¢ or $1. Every time I taught a class, I learned more. I learned what words helped explain things in a way that people could understand, I learned what words were not so effective, and I kept refining my language.

Each week I added more to the little booklet until I saw it turn into a book. I thought that maybe I could make some money on it. At the same time, someone asked if she could study finger cymbals with me. Again I started putting out a few lesson plans, and since much of the music theory for the finger cymbals is the same as for drums, I wrote both books during the same year.

I was starting to perform at about that time. Since I hadn't studied with any one teacher long enough to have a particular style, I created my own style, which is a lot of me mixed in with techniques I've picked up all over the country.

By that time, belly dancing had become quite popular. There were certain areas where conventions were held with 200 or 300 people in attendance. The music seemed very mystical to them. They thought that because the music was Middle Eastern, somehow you couldn't apply Western musical notation to it or you'd lose the spirit. But Western musical notation *does* apply to the rhythmic aspect of Middle Eastern music (not to the melodic aspect, because the melodies are more complicated). Two plus two equals four. Whether you're in China or Egypt or the United States, you count music the same way. I decided to take the chance that dancers would be serious enough to want to learn music theory from scratch so that they could understand the music. I used Western notation—quarter notes, eighth notes, 4/4 time, etc.—and I made it work in the Middle Eastern music world. I tried to illuminate an area that had been regarded as dark and mystical.

I hired four people to assist me with the production of the books: an editor skilled in the English language, a proofreader, a friend who knew all about layout, and an artist who took photos of my hands in various positions and then drew them so that I'd have illustrations along with the verbal explanations. I didn't have any money, so I borrowed $1,500 from my parents. I knew I could make money with the books once they were printed. One of my uncles owns a printing company, and I arranged to pay him so much down and the rest in payments.

It occurred to me that it would be much easier for people to learn from the books if they could match the visual examples to an actual drum demonstration they could listen to, so I made cassette tapes to accompany the books. Certainly it's better to learn from a teacher, but if there is no teacher a book and a tape are much better than just listening to the music and trying to figure out what to do.

After I made companion tapes to go with the drum and cymbal books, I decided to make a beginning instruction cymbal tape that doesn't have any accompanying book. I figured that some people prefer to have lessons given to them verbally. Then just six months ago, I came out with a practice music tape. It's the first time I've included melody.

By now I've played with most of the well-known Middle Eastern musicians throughout the United States. On top of having to deal with their feelings about women doing things besides housework, I have to break through the Middle Eastern/Anglo barrier. When my sponsor says, "We've got this great woman drummer in from San Francisco who wants to sit in and play with your band, can she do that?" the response is often one of great skepticism: "O.K., since you're her sponsor and this is your show, we'll let this little girl beat the drum a bit and then we'll go about our business." When I get up there and pick up my drum, they are very attentive to see what I'm going to do. Usually after the first or second piece, though, they sit back, and by the end of the night they're asking me, "Mary Ellen, can you stay here longer and join our band?" I've learned a tremendous amount by playing with these musicians.

Not long ago, I met Anthony Cirone, the percussionist with the San Francisco Symphony. After I sent him my books and tapes, he asked me to be a guest lecturer on Middle Eastern percussion at San Jose State University. One day I said, "Tony, you know you're a composer and you like my music. How about if I give you a crash course in Middle Eastern rhythms and you make a composition based on them but using Western symphonic instruments. I'll be a soloist in it." He took me up on that. So I put together tapes of the rhythms and sounds that he should be familiar with, and he read my books, and in a few months he was ready to write a composition.

We structured the piece together. Then Tony orchestrated it for a nine-piece percussion ensemble. We did the world premiere at San Jose State and had a professional make a tape of it. *Cairo Suite* takes about 20 minutes to perform. Eventually we hope to include it in an album.

Then George Mundy and I were given the honor of playing the music for the opening of the King Tut exhibit here in San Francisco, which was attended by 500 invited guests, including Governor Brown, Senator Cranston, the Egyptian ambassador to the U.S., and a delegation from Cairo who came over expressly to attend the opening. We were paid well, and it has led to other performances.

Now besides playing for private parties, and selling my drum and cymbal books through my own mail order business, I teach classes in my home and give seminars around the country. If there is a good turnout at a seminar, I can make close to $1,000 through a combination of teaching and selling.

I'd like to make enough money so that I can justify not going out and getting a 9-to-5 job, as I need self-fulfillment as well as money. It's self-fulfilling for me to bring all my talents together: the music, the teaching, the writing, and the social aspects. I entertain a lot. Musicians and dancers from all over the country come here. Now I'm getting to know some of the prominent Egyptians in town, like the consul general and his wife and the curator of the King Tut exhibit. I enjoy entertaining such people, and it's nice to incorporate the social aspects as part of my work.

My husband is very supportive of what I do, but he has some strong feelings about balancing my attention between my business and my family. I'm practicing my drum here at home so I'm seemingly accessible, yet I'm not actually accessible because I'm saying, "Don't bother me." At one point he said, "You just have to give some more attention to John and me. You can't be running this business in our home every day from 8:00 in the morning to midnight." And I really do feel better when I can put energy into my family as well as into my business.

My secretary, Jo Horton, helps me to do that because she's a total helper. She does the bookkeeping and the secretarial work, mails out the orders, does my grocery shopping and housekeeping, including the cleaning and the dishes, and plants the gardens. We work well together and are, of course, in constant contact.

I don't want to go back into the counseling world at this time. My heart is in the music and I want to make money at it—I *have* to bring in some money just so we can live comfortably—but I have to be realistic. It may not be possible to make this business big enough to be profitable. Besides, the belly dance enthusiasm is waning, and I can't say that in five years this will be making money for me. Several universities are incorporating full courses in Middle Eastern music. Ethnomusicology is becoming accepted as a genuine area of study, so with that happening on the college level, there might be opportunities there.

For information regarding instructional manuals and cassette tapes write: Mary Ellen Books, P.O. Box 7589, San Francisco, California 94120.

Jocelyn Levitt

FREE-LANCE PASTRY CHEF TO FINE
RESTAURANTS AND GOURMET CATERER,
Louisville, Kentucky.

*About two-fifths of the women we interviewed operated home busi-
nesses that were subject to deadlines, such as producing sufficient
work to sell at craft fairs or meeting schedules imposed by clients.
Although organization might increase efficiency, it cannot eliminate
stress, which is an integral part of these businesses.*

There's a lot of emotional stress in this business, and there's
always pressure. When we're doing a party for 400 people, there's
all the food to prepare, and good food should not be prepared *way*
in advance. Some of it has to be prepared fresh. And there is that
departure time when everything has to be packed up and you have
to get everything out. If you know you are not the only ones going
through all this, you can take it a whole lot better.

For a long time, I gave away nearly everything I cooked and baked.
I'm a compulsive cook, and I had to do something with the food. We
couldn't eat it all, although we tried. We just gave it away because I
like doing it, and the things I was doing it for were always nice things,
for people who were having parties or for celebrations.

At one point I decided that I wanted to overcome my compulsive cooking and change my personality. I was reading a book that I thought would help me, and my beauty operator said,

"What are you reading?"

I said, "Psycho-cybernetics."

"What's that?"

"Well, I'm going to change my personality, and I'm going to come out like Rita Hayworth."

"Who's that?" she asked. That shows you how young she was and how old I was. The woman in the chair next to mine, a psychiatrist, laughed with us and said, "Jocelyn, what are you doing that for? You're a successful woman." I'd been president of a women's service organization in town.

"I have this compulsion to bake and cook," I said, "and I've got to stop."

"Don't stop doing something that you're accomplished at," she said. "You're approaching it wrong. Think of it another way. Instead of eating it, continue to produce it, but open a tea shop or take it to a place where it can be sold. That's how to solve your problem." With that in mind, I was ready, and shortly after that, an opportunity came for me to begin.

I made a special Passover cake for a friend, and her brother-in-law, who had dinner there, later recommended me to a man who was opening a restaurant and needed a pastry chef. He tested me by asking me to make certain things, such as a coconut cream pie, a chocolate cake, and a loaf of bread (one I'd won a blue ribbon for). I was so petrified and so nervous that day that I decided that Morton, my husband, had better come with me. Besides, Morton knew about prices and I didn't.

The whole time the restaurant owner was tasting things, Morton kept saying, "That's not the best thing she makes. You should taste the chocolate pie she makes." The man hired me.

I learned more from that man! Although he no longer has the restaurant, I talk to him every time I need advice. He was very patient and explained all those things that can be cut in a restaurant and keep its shape, and all those things that don't spoil, and all the things that people like. We worked together for two years until his restaurant closed. Then, for a time, I prepared pastries for a four-star restaurant here in town that is touted as the poshest restaurant in Louisville.

When I went into business, I didn't need to borrow money because the house came with two kitchens, and I used the regular equipment that I had. Later, when I added equipment, I financed myself from Morton's realty business before he quit to join me in catering. We expanded when we could afford to—when we knew the business was there—not because of a nice piece of equipment that we'd like to have. When we bought this large convection oven, we had the business to fill it at that time.

When I started doing the purchasing, I immediately went into places where I thought I could get wholesale prices, and when I had difficulty I thought they were discriminating against me because I was a woman. It turned out, however, that such places usually have a minimum amount they'll deliver for. It was difficult for me to physically haul the cases of ingredients. Now it's a chore for Morton, but it's a challenge for him, too, to find out where the best buy is and come home with a really good deal. For me it was get the ingredients and to hell with the price!

Women who have tried to do what I do ask me about costs—and costs are the problem. Also, a number of restaurants who use our pastries did not know how to price their things at first. When we cost-account a recipe, we go through every single ingredient, including even salt and half a teaspoon of vanilla, because whenever we make more than one of anything we find out that pretty soon we're using half a cup of vanilla, which represents a certain amount of money. Overhead and labor and various other things must be figured in. And for a job that I'm quoting six months ahead of time, I have to raise my prices a certain percentage for inflation.

Before I could put my food into a restaurant, I had to be inspected. I contacted the health department and said that I was supplying restaurants, so please come inspect me. The difficulty at first was that there were no printed rules and regulations to which I could comply. I found out when things changed and new rules and regulations were put into force only when inspectors arrived and told me I was in violation. Really, though, there's so little that can go wrong. We have great inspections. The man comes in, looks around with a flashlight in all the corners, asks if my thermometers are in the refrigerators, which they are, and he says, "Fine."

We always plan at least 24 hours in advance, depending on the calendar. We know that we'll be making large deliveries on Tuesday and Friday. We know that Saturday and Sunday are days on which we're going to cater parties. Depending on the time of the year, we know that we're going to have an extra demand for a certain kind of cake or pie, such as Derby pie on Derby Day. We can't predict when the weather will turn bad and business will therefore be slow. We do know that the day after the weather turns good, we're going to be extremely busy. Those are things you can't plan for.

One thing that we require when we're catering a large affair is that we do *all* the food. If we were to get associated with others, it would be hard for the consumer to differentiate and say, "Well, Jocelyn did the quiche but not the salad." They're going to think I did the salad, too, and if the salad isn't up to snuff, I get the blame.

Quality becomes a way of life, yet avoiding substitutes isn't easy. For example, we have to buy chocolate chips in little tollhouse bags because bakers' suppliers sell chocolate-flavored pieces, not real chocolate chips. Nowadays there are substitutes even for substitutes. Bakers use a chemical derivative of corn syrup instead of sugar. The substitute for chocolate is actually granulated molasses. And everything is machine done. An upright and a horizontal bar on an icing machine assure that cakes come out perfect, but the icings cannot be made with whipping cream and butter, which ours are, because they have to be firm and stiff.

What does the lack of quality in the baking industry really mean for the future way of life? Does it make a difference? Is what we are doing antiquated? It becomes a matter of who can afford to buy these pastries. I'm thankful that the kind of catering that we do is not the only thing we do, because if I had to make a living just catering, I'd be doing a different kind of catering. I'd have to make the beef-pot-pie kind of food in order to stay in business.

When we had expanded this business and had outgrown the house, we started to look for another place, and we found out it was not readily available. That prompted us to decide to go into the restaurant business.

After our restaurant is open, we will continue to supply it from home with the same kind of food that we're supplying to restaurants now—with some additional things, of course. We'll have a 64-seat capacity. We can keep quality control by keeping it small. We'd have to buy too many processed foods if we got too large because we'd be beyond what our own capacity enabled us to prepare.

In the fall of 1978, JOCELYN'S opened at 9944 Linn Station Road, Plainview Center, Kentucky, and a year later the restaurant had expanded to a capacity of 110.

A tennis shop in back of us went bankrupt, so we took over that space. We've added a wine bar and created a more intimate atmosphere in the new room. We also expanded the kitchen, so now I do everything from the restaurant. Since we've hired more help, although I work the same hours from sunup to sundown, I no longer do the detailed work myself. Tomorrow, for New Year's Eve, we'll be serving a seven-course champagne dinner.

Coralee S. Kern

MAID SERVICE BUSINESS OWNER,
Chicago, Illinois.

Several of the women expressed frustration over people's belittling reactions to their home businesses. It was somehow assumed that they were not really serious about their endeavors, and consequently some of the women were self-conscious about revealing that their businesses were run from home.

When I started this business, several publications wanted to write stories about me, but I wouldn't allow it. I couldn't tell people that I was working from home. That wouldn't come out of me. I couldn't say it just as I couldn't say that my husband had deserted me when our children were little.

I needed money. The doctor had told me that I'd be unable to go out and work any more, and I knew I'd need additional money to pay doctor bills and for my two youngsters on their way to college. I was speaking to my mother on the telephone about my interest in starting a maid service, and the name of the company came to her right away. She said, "I think you should call it Maid to Order. Your Blue

Chip Maid Service." That day I decided that I'd go into the business, and I did.

I sent letters to maid services across the country. I told them that my husband was being transferred and was moving to the city and wanted to find out if they had a daily maid service. I was stunned at what I received in reply. Some of the services didn't even have stationery. They'd take business cards and scratch out and write things in. That really convinced me of the need for a good service. I also picked up a lot of ideas. For instance, some of the services would sign up a client to a contract for a year to clean their apartment every week.

I registered the name of my business with the State of Illinois, took the money out of my savings account, and started a bank account. I selected an answering service that I thought could really front for me so that nobody would know I was working from home. I went to great pains to do that. That was really one of the most difficult jobs that I did because I was so sick. I hired an artist to design a logo for me. Then I started to do things like try to get people to sell me stationery so I could send out a mailing.

People were convinced that I was crazy. Nobody wanted to come to sell me anything, because I didn't have a business yet, and especially because I was working from home. My young son Kevin, who was 15 at that time, had to complete some of the arrangements for me because people were reluctant to come and see me. He also interviewed potential employees. My children knew that I was sick, and they new that my money was limited. Without Kevin, I wouldn't have this business. I've gotten all the glory from it.

I realized a good service would have to take the woman doing the work into consideration as much as the client. So we started out on that basis. We made it very clear to our clients how important our domestic workers were to us.

I've always been interested in women who were alone, because I *was*, and women who were poor, because I *was*, and so I had made an independent study of domestic workers and their lot in life, and I was really as interested in the domestic worker as I was in the service.

The only way that the domestic worker can ever begin to create and make any change in her life is if she has steady employment—not just employment at the whim of a customer—if she *knows* she's going to work 30 to 40 hours a week all the time and that she will be paid. We've made our clients understand through our service that we all have a responsibility to what's happening to the women who really want to go out and work and who really don't want to stay on welfare.

Ninety-nine percent of our women live in very marginal neighborhoods and they have a lot of concerns about leaving their children alone and getting home late, so we don't want to send them too far. We figure out how long it's going to take a person to get back and forth. Their time is as valuable as ours.

We offer our women eight hours work, but most domestic workers work about five and a half or six hours. Every single person has a different idiosyncrasy and a different story to tell, and I wouldn't have a business had I not listened to why they couldn't do this or that. Many women work for us different days and different schedules because of clinic appointments. Every hospital in Chicago runs a special clinic for black women and blood pressure. Half of our women can't work because they're going to a clinic. That's the kind of thing that you have to understand. Or they have a child that has a learning disability or any number of other things.

You cannot run this kind of a business without being tied up into the feelings domestic workers have and the kinds of problems they have. It's true that some maids are undependable, but it's also true that a lot of women have problems that are just unbelievable. I can't tell you how many women who have worked for us in this service have daughters who have been raped. I just can't tell you how many. And the women live in apartments where the back porch falls off or the ceiling falls in. I always said that I was poor. I was never that poor. It's just unbelievable the kinds of experiences that our women have. One woman just this week could not get to work because there's a flasher in her neighborhood and she has two little girls that she sends to school. She's been taking them back and forth to school.

Since I've been in business, I've been named next of kin for people who have gone into the hospital. At that point, I realized what the women were feeling. I'm always here because this is my home and my business. It's a form of real stability to them. We have over 300 employees now.

I wanted to gear the business to certain areas in the city where there were blocks of money. We used the voter registration poll sheets from very exclusive buildings, and we sent them the mailing. That put us in business right away.

At the same time that the people were calling us to give us orders or to inquire about our service, my son was interviewing domestic workers downtown in an office we rented for $50 a month. He would bring the applications home and we would go over them. He was a very stern, critical 15-year-old, and it used to bother me to hear some of the things that he said. But now that I look back I think that's one of the things that helped us, because we selected the best.

We were interested in women who knew the difference in working for a paycheck as opposed to cash. We wanted to work with people who had cleaning references, and we did verify their references. We received a lot of clients that way. People were so pleased that we had sent a reference letter on an old domestic worker of theirs that they asked us to send them our literature, which we did.

We were interested in whether or not a woman was dependable and reliable, whether or not if she took a commitment she'd get to work, whether or not she was experienced in doing all types of housework, because we didn't want to deal with women who said, "I only iron, I'm only a laundress." In our business, you need a multipurpose woman to do housework. And I really wanted women who knew how to clean. I knew then that I'd have fewer charge-offs for things that they might break. We needed women who we were sure did not drink, and we wanted to be sure that our women were honest.

When I first went into the business. I spoke with the captain of the police department close to a very wealthy area in Chicago, and asked him what kinds of experiences I could expect. He told me that I wouldn't have to be worried about maid theft because black women, with whom I deal, usually are not thieves, but, one thing for sure, some rich folks are liars. It has turned out to be true.

Many people will set maids up for thievery, and will maintain that their ring is gone or their coat is gone, to try to get the insurance out of it. I was totally unsophisticated in dealing with these kinds of problems, but I protected myself with insurance, and we purchased a bond.

A bond doesn't really mean very much because somebody has to be convicted of a crime in order to really get money back on a bond. If you called me up and said, "The maid took my color television set," I'd say to you, "I'm really sorry that happened. You *must* call the police department." The police have to apprehend the woman and we will cooperate with them. The woman has to be brought to court and found guilty before the bonding company pays. In fact, that just doesn't happen. When people found out that I had a bond, they would never even go to the police. If it got as far as the police, I would be told, "Now this is the seventh time there's been a problem in that apartment since I've been in this police district."

If something is suspect, we don't give a woman a second chance, and I explain that to each woman when I hire her. I feel I have to have some form of protection for myself. If a client calls up and says, "The maid did a terrible job," I use the maid again because a terrible job to you might not be a terrible job to your neighbor. And a maid may not do one particular job well. There's a difference in how maids perform.

I went out and cleaned apartments and set criteria for what would be done. We did after-construction cleaning and then cleaning in model apartments. We used different products in each apartment so we knew which one cleaned the best. We established a pretty good idea of how long it should take. We've gotten to a point where if we're not allowed enough time, we won't take the job, because I don't want the complaints.

We interview an average of 35 women before we hire one. We also have a few men who work for us. When I started the business it never occurred to me that I'd have a man working for me, because I was sick and I hardly ever got dressed. I began to hire men to do some heavier, after-construction cleaning in a large high-rise. We would get contracts to clean 800 apartments before people moved in.

Sometimes people come to us who just need money to tide them over until they finish college or a training course. If we have a particular job that would fit their needs (like a one-time cleaning job of model apartments, a decorator showroom, or that kind of thing), I hire them. It's better in our business if you try to send the same domestic worker to a home, particularly if both people are working, because then the cleaning woman knows their home and works better and faster and the clients feel better because a lot of people aren't going in and out of the house.

We clean homes and apartments in Chicago and in the suburbs, generally on an every-week or every-other-week basis.

That's a large percentage of our business. Another *big* business that we're doing is that of cleaning corporate apartments. Large companies have luxury apartments in Chicago for chairmen of the board or for important people who come from foreign countries. And some wealthy people who live in the suburbs maintain apartments so when they come to the symphony, for example, they can stay downtown. We go in and maintain these like hotel rooms.

I've really learned a lot. I began to realize that the more hours I booked in this business did not necessarily mean more profit. My accountant told me that all the time. If it wouldn't have been for this magnificent old man who was willing to take all the time in the world to show me all these things, I just wouldn't have made it. I really feel that he's responsible.

The first thing we did was put our payroll on an every-other week instead of an every-week basis. Next was to charge a dollar an hour more for any client that we billed. We told all of our clients to leave a check in the apartment, that the woman who cleaned the apartment would pick it up, put it in an envelope we gave to her, and mail it here, which meant that we got our money immediately and didn't have to bill the client; and I was able to get rid of a woman who spent 36 hours a week typing bills. It made a fantastic difference in terms of my cash.

Also, I was serving anybody, anywhere, for any amount of time, which is stupid. Why should a woman go to Evanston and work three hours and then trot on another two buses and work three hours someplace else? That's an abuse of her time. We now have a three-hour minimum for clients who live in buildings where we do a lot of business, so we can have a woman go in and do two three-hour customers, which would be six hours. Then she goes home. From the standpoint of scheduling people on that basis, we've noticed an increase in our profits. It was clear and simple.

Our party catering service began shortly after a client was going to have a party. I sent her a woman who unfortunately did not do a good job at her party. The client called me to tell me what the woman did wrong, and I wrote down all the things she said the woman should have done. I thanked her very much, and I never sent her a bill for that woman's services—and I went into the party business.

Several caterers we work with cater the food and we provide

labor. We go in and help them set up, serve, and clean up. We advertise that people should be guests at their own party. Many people who use us on New Year's Eve send in the money to pay for this year's party as well as a deposit to reserve one of our people for next year.

When I started this business, I didn't realize that the timing was so good. There's no question that with women going back to work in order to maintain any kind of standard of living, more and more people will be using services, because women just will not do everything any more. That's one of the big changes that we've noticed recently. The average income of our clients is lower than it was when we started. Working wives can't keep up with everything, and husbands are apparently reluctant to help. It's not unusual for men to call us to make arrangements.

We intend to license our business. We're giving people the right to use our name, our slogans, our logo, and all the information we have copyrighted. We're going to sell consulting services to them for a period of years. We've outlined what we want in our operating manual, and we're taking bids now from people to write it for us. I expect that we'll have quite a few other offices by the end of the year. That's going to be really exciting. Years ago I was a franchise coordinator, and I happen to know a great deal about setting up multiple offices and getting them working.

This is a much needed business. It's a well organized business. It's a very profitable business. When I started it, I never felt I was going to fail. I never thought that I'd do *this* well, and I certainly never thought that I'd have people pursuing me, wanting to take this idea and go further with it.

After I started the business in October 1972, I was in the hospital. By the time the business was really going, everybody was calling me. It was a really big hassle to try to operate the business when I was in the hospital. There were many times when I begged to stay clear of drugs so I could sign paychecks. That's how bad it's been. I've been in the hospital a lot. I really feel very sensitive about it. It's a very negative part of my life. I fought a battle to live. Not financially—physically. I *really* fought a battle to live. It was a terrible, terrible time for me.

I love this baby. That's what it is, it's a baby. I really *love* this business because it did lots of things to me. At the same time that this all happened, my daughter went away to college and I happen to be very close to my children and I thought I'd die. I *really* and truly thought I'd die. I can remember that feeling as though it was yesterday. It was one of the worst days of my life when I saw her go.

The business means a lot to me because it gave me the opportunity to live—not just financially. Everybody discouraged me except my mother. They just thought you don't make money from home, you can't make money if you're sick, you can't be dependable yourself, you can't be reliable. "You can never make it with black women. No way are you going to get your maids, Coralee." I just could not believe the things that people said to me. But even more important than just the money that I've made in the business to keep myself going is that I really found something I like to do. I like the women who work in the service. It's added a different dimension to my life. And my clients have been absolutely marvelous. Had it not been for a couple of very wealthy women in this city who paid me months in advance, I would never have made it.

One time when I was very sick in the hospital, my mother came up and she answered the telephone: "Now I'm returning your phone call. I'm sorry Coralee is very sick and *if* she makes it"—and there was a chance as to whether or not I would make it—"we'll call and let you know if the business is still going to be running." Apparently she said this so calmly and matter-of-factly that people kept calling back to see whether or not I was going back into business, and I never lost a client, even though they had to keep their houses clean. I'm sure they used other services while I was hospitalized. When I was able to function again, I hired somebody else to back me up in case anything ever happened, and I never had that problem again.

One day you can think your life is over in every way possible, physically and financially and emotionally, and your kids are gone, and the next day, or two or three weeks later, it looks different. It's very interesting.

On March 23-24, 1979, the first Chicago Women's Career Convention was held. Thousands of women attended. The Yellow Pages, *the convention's guide book, included articles, a listing of the seminars and workshop offerings, and the following dedication:*

Coralee has devoted much of her time and energy towards women's programs. She serves on the Illinois Commission on the Status of Women and has been active in promoting women as business owners. Because Coralee is truly an example of a woman who has made it, we are dedicating the effort we put into publishing The Yellow Pages to her. Thanks, Coralee, for your help and inspiration.

For information write: Coralee Kern, Maid to Order, 224 South Michigan Avenue, Chicago, Illinois 60604.

Rosemary James

PUBLICIST AND LOBBYIST,
New Orleans, Louisiana.

Most of the women we interviewed were satisfied to work from home, and those without children found their increased productivity a major asset. Safety was another factor they considered an advantage in working from home.

Basically I want to keep myself busy on the work scene 50 to 60 hours a week. It's easier to put that much work in if I'm working at home because I don't waste a lot of time getting all dolled up and commuting to a central business district unless I have to see a client. It's only when I'm in a business meeting that I'm called on to turn myself out in a fancy way.

I go to the typewriter and start working many mornings before I ever open my shutters for business. I let everybody know that I'm really not open until 10:00. That means I can get a lot of work out early in the morning. I also find that if I'm really doing something creative, I may go on till midnight. If I were in an office, I might not feel so secure.

When I decided to go into business for myself, I'd been a political reporter at WWL-TV for about eight years. I started looking for a way to improve my business skills, but I couldn't quite understand how I was going to learn how to do things like figuring out a budget.

That fall of 1976 I went to Russia with two other people as guests of the Soviet government through a local outfit, International House. During the trip, one of them, the port director of the Port of New Orleans, who was an old friend of mine, mentioned that his organization needed some help and told me that when I got ready to leave my TV reporting position, he'd like to talk to me.

When I got back, I became so disgusted with the lack of technical cooperation on the film series I was trying to get out on Russia that I called him and said, "I'm ready to leave. What can you offer me?"

The Dock Port was looking for someone to run its legislative liaison program, and since all my contacts while at WWL-TV were primarily political, I was hired at a pretty good salary. They wanted $75,000,000 for bonds from the legislature over a period of five years, and I got it in the first session.

The Port position was really exciting, to find that I could go to Baton Rouge and immediately jump the fence and have the legislators treat me as somebody who could lobby them. I'd been covering them for eight years—even longer, really, as a newspaper reporter before that. At first they were a little bit nervous, because they still thought of me as a reporter, but it didn't take long to get across what I was doing, and they were really cooperative. It's a great feeling to find that you can convert one talent to another.

The Dock Port position was an absolute godsend because I was given a department of my own and I had to learn to make up a budget. It's all set up so that you can learn it according to the state forms, including how to purchase supplies and all the stuff so necessary in running a business.

The Dock Board really didn't have a public information department, just a lot of different people doing things in that area, so I organized the department. When I got through with that, there really wasn't a lot of challenge left.

I definitely knew I wanted to go into public relations and/or lobbying, with some advertising on the side. My first bout out as a lobbyist, I felt I'd done pretty well, so I figured maybe I could do it for somebody else—this is the time I'm either going to do it or I'm never going to do it. I started looking for some accounts, and I immediately came up with two solid clients.

I took on, as my very first account, the Strachan Shipping Company, one of the oldest, most successful steamship agencies in the community. It didn't really need product-oriented advertising and PR. What it needed instead was institutional advertising to modernize its image while emphasizing its tradition. The Strachan people like to joke that I'm dragging them into the 20th century hollering and screaming all the way. They weren't getting free publicity for their services because nobody was handling it, yet they had good feature stories that could be developed, describing a new service from one point to another point—for example, from New Orleans to West Africa—that was of news interest. The thing to do is keep a client's name before the shipping public as much as possible, and any kind of feature story that can be developed that has an angle of the service it provides is worth the effort. For example, if it can handle a cargo in a special way, better than somebody else, you want to get that placed in a medium like *The Port Record*, a magazine that goes to 20,000 people interested in shipping.

It's up to a publicist to come up with something that has some news value as well as promotional value to the client. You can get more out of it if you featurize it a little bit. I find that if the story is well written, it has an element of news, and if I send some excellent photographs, the story will be used. The photographs are *very* important. My policy has always been to not bug my media sources with stuff that has no real value. Once in a while I have to send out these business office things, but I tell the people at the newspaper or wherever, "Use it if you can, but it's not going to hurt my feelings if you don't."

Another aspect of my PR business is to provide clients with sales tools, something that will help them when they're calling on their clients. One Strachan brochure, for instance, was designed primarily for a European ship owner who doesn't know a lot about the ports of Jacksonville, New Orleans, Mobile, and others. We had a map done for each port to show what facilities there were. We included a little information about each port, aiming primarily at facilities that would be of interest to tramp operators. Since tramp operators offer their ships on charter wherever cargo is available, they're interested in bulk facilities, oil terminals, and general cargo stuff. Generally we wanted to give Strachan Shipping Company a tool its salesmen could use when they called on tramp owners. It had to be modern, fairly slick, but not so expensive that it looked like a lot of money was being wasted. Other sales tools of interest to my clients are slide and video tape presentations, films, brochures, and direct mail campaigns.

The second account I took on was a rather controversial financier—an oil man, a banker, a real estate man, and an insurance man—a legend in his own time and somebody I've always been very interested in as a human being. I felt he could use a little public relations because of his controversial nature. So I went to him, and he agreed.

Those were nice accounts and provided my base. Because I had been with WWL-TV for quite a long time, and because I had been with the Dock Board for a short time, I had accumulated some pension refunds. I didn't have to borrow any money from anybody.

I started out in a second-floor apartment. One of my clients offered me some office space to help me get started, but all the people I talked to in the business advised me to keep my overhead low and told me I could do without an office, because in the public relations business you spend most of your time in the client's office. I grew out of that apartment pronto and started looking for a house.

I wanted *this* property really badly, and I bit off a lot, buying a house way beyond my means. French Quarter property is like blue-chip stock. Another thing I learned—and I didn't really need to learn it while I was also starting a business—was that I couldn't afford the luxury of paying 33% to a general contractor on top of very extreme renovation costs, so I subcontracted this house myself.

Everybody told me not to count on the business breaking even for at least six months and probably not for a year. But I broke even after the first two months, paying myself a salary, and by the end of the year I had paid myself back all the money I had lent the business. Then I borrowed money out of the business to help with this house. The business has not only provided me with a living, it's become my bank.

Now I do advertising as well as public relations, but only for a few clients who have me on a public relations retainer. I'm not at all interested in getting into the retail advertising business. That requires a lot of overhead. You almost have to have your own artist and media buyer—things of that nature. That means you get into extra personnel, taxes, all kinds of overhead expenses that are really needed in a retail advertising business. Advertising is feast-and-famine, too. You'll have a big account one day, and the next thing you know you're told your stuff is not very creative and you're out the window. You've geared up for this big account, and you've got to fire everybody. I know an agency that was given a tremendous amount of work but lost two big accounts and had to fire everybody. It's an agonizing thing. Whereas in public relations you're charging primarily for your personal services, and you can make more money without having to spend so much on physical layout. If you've only got a secretary and you're farming out all your creative work, you have the advantage of being able to cut back, tighten your belt if you lose an account, and go out and look for another one immediately without the agony of having to fire people.

So that I have time to service all my accounts in a professional manner, I try to keep my clients varied between accounts that are going to need a lot of service on little things and accounts that need consulting advice but not so much detail work. I don't believe in keeping an account unless I can service it, because I don't want to build a reputation for doing nothing for my clients. I just got an enormous account, and I had to resign a couple of little ones because I wouldn't be able to handle them properly.

There's a huge tract of land in New Orleans called New Orleans East, Inc., which represents half of all the undeveloped land left in the city. It's been idle for 20 years. The ownership is changing, and they're getting ready to create a new town project that's going to take 25 years to develop.

I was recommended to them by a man in the market research business who has represented them for years in other developments. He kept asking me to write a series of confidential memos on various aspects of the city which, he said, "may or may not develop into some business, but if you do this for me, I'd appreciate it." That's the way I got the account.

It turned out that they were bringing in as project manager a very brilliant man from Australia who's not at all familiar with the local scene, and the memos were to bring him up to date quickly on areas of specific concern—everything to do with the public sector. For instance, what did I see as the problems with the ports? There are a number of archeological sites that have to be preserved. Corridors for future rapid transit need to be protected. Coastal zone management is a very big issue in this state right now, and I'm representing them in that area. All kinds of reports have to be gone through to see if they have a bearing on the project and how devastating they might or might not be. The developers are sensitive people, and they want to make sure that they don't do anything to hurt anybody, but at the same time they don't want to be blocked unreasonably in developing property. Since I had covered Louisiana politics, legislators, and other public officials for 14 years, they are friends of mine, people I know on a first-name basis, which makes the contact work with them easy for me. I'm not exactly lobbying them because they're not really asking for anything—they're just clearing the way. That is my principal activity with New Orleans East for the time being.

It's going to be an enormous project—27,000 acres of land, 8,000 acres of which are wetlands outside the levee-protection system that are never going to be developed, plus residential, commercial, recreational, and industrial sites. Essentially, it's going to be creating a new city in the only direction that New Orleans has left to expand in any major way. New Orleans desperately needs good light manufacturing, because we have an incredibly high rate of unemployment. Beyond that, there's a growing need for public relations on behalf of the City of New Orleans and of New Orleans East in order to solicit European investment in industrial ventures. It's really very challenging to me to be involved in the future of the city.

Because I've bitten off more than I can chew, I sometimes end up working 18 hours a day. I don't mind, right now especially, because it's really challenging me, and it's important to me to make this business go. And so far it's going very well.

Some of my clients have put me on set retainers, so I'm guaranteed a certain amount of income. For others I work on a $50-an-hour basis, and so obviously the more work I do for them, the more money I'm going to make. I've learned not to depend on them for a certain amount of income. I must be very careful when I accept a client, first of all, to have faith that they're going to pay—but I don't go on faith alone. I don't do anything for political clients unless I'm paid in advance, because I don't care how good they are, if they lose, and there's no money in the till, it's going to be hard to collect. Everyone in this business has a code word called CIA—Cash In Advance for politicians.

I have a contract of some sort, a letter of agreement, with all my clients. For clients like Strachan, I have a little sheet called a contact report, and I fill it out and say what I did. At the end of the month, I submit the contact reports along with my bill, and if there's any question, the details are right there in front of them.

It's very important for me to have two or three clients who provide a set amount of money that guarantees my overhead and salary so that I'm not worried where my next meal is coming from and so I can really address my attention to improving the business. Then everything else that comes in beyond that begins to look pretty nice. At that point, I can figure out how much of this I want to keep and how much of my life I want to spend working.

Frances Gabe

INVENTOR AND ARTIST,
Newberg, Oregon.

Fourteen of the women we interviewed lived alone. Nine were engaged in service businesses, and five were artists. Frances Gabe, an inventor and artist, felt that living alone finally gave her the opportunity to excel in the pursuit of her life's work—inventing a self-cleaning home.

After I was alone, oh, gosh, I just gloried in that. That was heavenly! Ohhh! So many people thought I'd die of loneliness, but I didn't have time to be lonely. I hardly went out for anything except groceries and working materials, and I'd rush back here and get to work again. It was the most exciting thing I'd ever done in my life—absolutely the most thrilling. You have no idea how excited I was about the self-cleaning house. And then when something I'd worked on for weeks finally jelled, I'd be so high I'd work all day and all night. Sometimes I'd work 36 hours straight. I couldn't quit. I'd lock up all the doors and take the phone off the hook. I'd give it heck, and feel so good.

I belonged to myself finally. I felt as though I were a human being instead of a piece of machinery or a tool to be used by whoever needed me more than they thought I needed myself. Always,

always, I had felt that somebody else owned me more than I owned myself.

My background had been building and architecture. My father was a builder/architect. There were six of us kids. I was the only one that favored Dad in the least. From the time I was 2 years old, I was on the construction job with him. I was in his lap nights when he'd do his drawing and his drafting. We were buddies.

I rode his shoulders on the job, and he'd give me a big swatch of his hair with each hand. Up on the girders we'd go. "Hang on, Frenchie! Hang on! Hang on!"

I thought it wonderful up there. The air was so clean. You could look down on all of the minutiae below and feel so darn superior and above it all.

When I grew up, I majored in art. I studied metal arts, sculpture, ceramics, painting, commercial drawing, dressmaking, tailoring, and dress design, and later creative writing.

Then I married.

During the depression there wasn't any work for anybody. The unions were very nasty about who would sponsor my husband, an electrical engineer. "If he doesn't have a sponsor, we can't let him in, and he can't work unless he's union!" Here was this great big 6 ' 3½ " man who couldn't get a job to save his soul. We picked dirt with the chickens.

When the war started, he was drafted to work in the shipyards because of his electrical engineering education, but after the war there were still no jobs to be had. When someone offered him a job for $85 a month, I said, "Criminy! Forget it!"and I started a building repairs company.

I began with a question-and-answering service. The do-it-yourselfers would call for directions on how to do jobs. I would answer them very honestly and tell them exactly how. They'd finally call back and say, "For heaven's sakes! Send a man over. I can't do this!"

My husband did all the jobs. In the beginning he said, "I don't know anything about building!" "It isn't difficult," I said, "I can tell you."

He'd phone 12, 14 times a day, "What do I do now?" Poor guy.

He called frantically one day: "The plaster keeps falling off! What do I do? The people here are going to think I'm crazy!" "Then you're dabbing it," I said. "You have to *smear* it! You don't dab it. Smear one trowelful into the other and be sure that you dampen your wall a little or it won't stick."

And that's the way we started.

I mention this because I think it's quite important for people to understand that I know what I'm talking about when I talk about construction. So many people think, "What does a woman know about building? How could she possibly build a self-cleaning house? She couldn't build a woodshed."

I know quite a bit about building.

I woke up blind when my first baby was born. I'd hemorrhaged very badly, and the blood vessels in my eyes had collapsed. I was told I'd never even see the face of my baby, but over a period of 18 years I did get my vision back. Now I have 20/20 vision with my glasses on. The blindness is what made me so orderly. I put things where they belong. It's no fun to find you've put sugar and cinnamon on the meat instead of salt and pepper because someone switched the containers.

I managed our construction repairs business for years. By the time it was really going well, I was taking 16, 18 calls a day and managing it by phone although I was very ill. Besides being blind and having other health complications, I had broken my back. At one time, I managed the whole show for six months from my bed, and I had to lie flat on my back all that time.

It's been a wild story, really. I had a home to take care of and two young children, a son and a daughter. That was one reason I couldn't go out on the job myself. Being blind was another reason. But people's resentment about a woman doing that sort of work was the biggest reason. You either struggle and come up or you go down. I didn't have it in me to go down. I didn't know where down was. The struggle has been pure hell. I think women need to know that. The struggle is what gave me the backbone to fight the inspectors. It's what gave me guts to keep on going when half the town was calling me nuts. "Any damn fool who tries to do something impossible like a self-cleaning house is crazy!"

After I became blind, I took up sculpting because it was something I could do without seeing. I went into ceramics and then, after quite a few years had gone by and I was able to see some, I did such things as making all the clothes for weddings. I remember the day I could really see. I stitched the sewing machine needle through my fingers three times, one time right after the other, because there was confusion between sight and touch. I sobbed and cried my frustration and pain. I hadn't anticipated that I would have to make an adjustment back to visual sight.

About this time, the incompatibility that had been developing over the years between my husband and myself had become increasingly more difficult to cope with. I began losing my faith in the religion I'd been raised with—no divorce no matter what. I realized I needed to build myself a studio so I could produce my work and become financially independent. So I bought a piece of property for $50 down and $5 a month, and two years later, I sold it for $2,500. I bought a lot in Portland the same way. I bought this place here in the country with the money I had realized from those two properties. Finally I could build myself a studio.

My son was now 17 and my daughter had gotten married. I came out here, and the first thing I did was have the spinal fusion I needed very badly. I told my husband that he could have my share of the building repairs business, and I didn't go back to Portland.

The cabin was really no more than a chicken coop. It wasn't finished inside. The plumbing was very inefficient, as was the electrical wiring. I finished it myself. I took the woodshed and revamped it into a live-in studio for me alone. It took me ten years because there wasn't any money. I used materials that my husband threw in the dump from the jobs he did in Portland. After it was livable, he moved in here with me. Our relationship didn't improve any, and finally I told him he could have our Portland home. I had to have this studio for myself alone. We got divorced.

The art work did not pay enough, although it was always of a quality that belonged in a museum. People hired special buses to bring the teachers to see my work, but nobody bought it. They did buy the ceramics, but there isn't enough money in ceramics to amount to a hill of beans. I worked with gypsum, cement, precious metals, resin, and oils.

I used to wonder why God let me go clear to the very point of success on so many things but something would happen to just sweep it away. Why, just when I began teaching art, did I go blind? It was that way again and again and again. Ceramics. O.K. Exceptional work. Wonderful quality. Considered an authority on clay, but there was no money in it. I'm always exceptional but I don't make it. Why?

I could see myself growing old and ending up in a rest home some place because nobody gave a darn. I'm too different. Someone like me sticks out like a sore thumb. If you're that different, the whole darn world is going to punish you some way. That's the way people are made, I think. I couldn't expect much help from very many sources.

John, an architect friend of mine, was married for just two years when his wife lost consciousness and stayed in a coma for the next two years. He kept her at home and took care of her. I watched John go to pieces and slowly die with his wife. After two years he had a heart attack and died. That's when I decided, "Well, by God! Something's going to give! This isn't going to happen any more!" I'd had a spinal fusion, but my broken back could never heal because I worked too hard. Enough is enough!

I decided that people like John were going to have a home that they could stay in no matter how old or sick they got. As long as they could punch a button, they could take care of themselves. A self-cleaning house (SCH) was my idea of a solution. They weren't going to have to move out because their homes were too big for them to take care of. They weren't going to be forced out of homes they had worked for all their lives.

Also, a self-cleaning house would be my gift to young mothers, because during all the years that my children were growing up, they were always wanting me to do things with them. I would always have to say I was sorry because I had to clean the blasted house, do the laundry, wash the dishes.

After I got the idea, I wondered, "Where do I begin? Where in the dickens is the starting point of this thing? Everything has got to coordinate. I've got to start somewhere." So, I figured it this way: What things drive me nuts about a house and housework? What things do I feel are terribly inefficient? What things take too doggone much time for the benefits you get out of them? I made a list of everything that annoyed me about keeping house. That was a simple matter for me.

I experimented a long time to find a medium that would clean all of the household soil. You can't use gasoline. You can't use solvent.

You can't use any of the things that you'd ordinarily use for heavy cleaning. And so I kept coming back to soap and water. There have been many comparatively self-cleaning homes, but they have belonged to the extremely wealthy, and they're electronically operated, and they don't remove sticky or greasy dirt. I wanted something that almost everyone could afford, something within the reach of the working woman and man. I decided it would have to be soap and water.

I figured the possibilities, thinking, "Yeah, yeah, yeah, flood the place." Well, you can't do that, so it had to be worked out.

I went to Oswego to the city engineer, at $50 an hour at that time. I managed to dig up the $50 to find out what water would do, how you handle water to do real cleaning without flooding a place. I had to know what size pipes and other materials to use. The engineer said, "Do you have *any idea* what you're talking about? Do you have any notion at all? Do you have the mental ability to even get the vaguest idea what this thing would *cost?*"

I said I thought I had a pretty good idea. Yes.

"Are you a wealthy woman?"

"No. I'm picking dirt with the chickens, but *I will do it!* I will do it."

"Good luck! But *why* don't you just go home and settle on inventing a new mayonnaise, lady?"

So I came home. It was blasted cold out—one of the meanest winters we've had. It was snowing and the wind was blowing, and oh, it was awful. I bundled up to the eyebrows and I went out to the old van we had sitting out here at that time. I deduced that there was every kind of dirt on that that I'd ever have to deal with in a house. We'd used it for a dog kennel for a time, then the kids used it for a play house. It had all the dirt in it you'd have in a house, besides a lot of rodent's lunch that had been sitting there for about two years.

I must've looked absolutely insane out there, spraying that darn thing with water, trying this and that apparatus, this and that gizmo, this and that temperature, this and that angle. If I couldn't do something the first time, I'd keep at it until I did. It isn't true, as many people think, that everything comes so bloody easy for me all the time. I sometimes have to do it over and over—and over yet again if need be. And that's how I managed to solve the myriad problems associated with the self-cleaning house.

I had invented a window block I call The Blushing Splendor,

which developed hairline cracks where the resin wall and the plastic glass window met. So the resin manufacturers sent me their specialist from California to be as much help as possible—at no cost to me. I asked him what would have caused the cracks, and I told him what my deductions were, and after he thought quite a while, he agreed with me but he had no solution. I had to solve that problem, and I did so. I want those blocks to go together so they can be used, instead of conventional walls, in any size opening, wherever you wish to use them.

I couldn't find any manufacturer on the entire West Coast who had the proper equipment to fabricate the blocks. People were very excited about them and wanted very much to make them, but nobody had anything big enough. The largest they could fabricate was 8", and I wanted the window blocks to be the same size as standard building blocks so builders can put one of them in a building without having to do a lot of cinder-block cutting. I'm a firm advocate of cinder blocks. I'm using them here because of the termites and carpenter ants in the forest surrounding my studio. Builders get really excited when they see these window walls; they think they're really neat things.

Another window block I invented, which I call Top Security, would make it impossible for anyone to break in anywhere it is used, except with a jackhammer. It would be marvelous for mental hospitals, prisons, warehouses, and for drug and pharmaceutical establishments. I think the windows would be perfect to put upstairs because you could leave them open and no child could possibly fall through.

People keep asking, "Where are the models that you worked on all this time? They've got to be fascinating. They belong in a museum." Heck almighty! Who could afford to keep them? I had to tear them apart to make new things out of them. For instance, I couldn't afford copper tubing to play with and throw away. So I tore the latest perfected inventions apart and used the pieces over again. And I finally came up with the apparatus that I will use. It has proved to be laboratory perfect. The final test will be how well it works in a full-scale model of the self-cleaning house I'm building as an apartment addition to the studio building.

Now I have 66 inventions ready to be fabricated and marketed. There's a closet-clothes freshener-combination. You hang your dirty clothes in the freshener on hangers, and you punch a button and go away. The next time you want your clothes, they're washed and dried and hanging in the closet. And why not? For the love of heaven, why take your clothes, put them in the washer, take them out of the washer, put them in a dryer, take them out of the dryer, fold them, and worry about doing it quickly enough so they don't wrinkle? After the clothes freshener has finished, your clothes are waiting for you without in any way affecting what was previously in your closet. The closet itself is self-cleaning because it is arranged so that the cleaning water from the freshener also cleans the floor of the closet, yet the floor is arranged so that whatever is sitting on it will remain untouched and won't be affected in any way by the cleaning. It's the arrangement that makes the difference.

And there's a dishwasher. You put the dirty dishes in the cupboard, punch a button, and when you take them out, they're washed and dried and ready to put on the table again. None of this business of putting them in the dishwasher, taking them out of the dishwasher, putting them in the cupboard, taking them out of the cupboard, and putting them on the table.

Then there's the therapeutic self-cleaning bathtub, which is eternally warm, if you so choose, and the self-cleaning washbasins, sink, and shower bath—and the rest of the bathroom, which is self-cleaning, every bit of it.

The present "labor savers" have kept women on their knees—not deliberately, though. It was convention that did it. There was no malicious intent in putting bathtubs low to the floor, but a woman can't even bathe a child without being on her knees. She can't scrub the toilet without being down with her face in the dirty thing. She's either on her knees or she has her head in a hole. Now just think about that a little bit. She's leaning over all the time, and I can't figure out why that is necessary. I can see why it was done that way originally. We have to begin someplace, but it is no longer necessary because we can go on from there. We can progress further still. I'm positive the SCH has done this.

I now know why all of my efforts before this had to fail even after I had become really good at whatever it was I was doing. I was training for what I would need to know before I could even begin to invent something that demanded as many different skills as the SCH has demanded. If I had succeeded with any one of them, I might have been content to stop right there. The SCH would never have been invented—at least not by me.

Juanita Bass

ANTIQUE DEALER,
Frankfort, New York.

Most of the women we interviewed preferred being left alone so that they could create their products undisturbed, or they brought companionship into their homes through their businesses. Moving her antique business from a downtown shop to her home gave Juanita Bass a sense of freedom.

I felt isolated when I had the shop downtown, because I'd sit there and wait for hours for someone to come, maybe to buy something so I could pay my rent. But being home, if I want to leave, I can. People said, "Well, gee, you're so far away." When someone wants something, they'll travel 200 or 300 miles, They know you have it. They'll come and get it.

My sister-in-law lives on a busy road and runs a garage sale all summer and does quite well. Tourists stop as they're driving through. One day she said to me, "Gee, you decided you wanted an antique shop and you did it. All of a sudden you've got your shop. You just go ahead and do things." And that's the way I am.

Sometimes I buy out estates, and in doing so I take *everything*. There's a lot of stuff you can sell and there's a lot of stuff you can't because it's just plain junk. It goes to the dump or you give it to a charity for an auction.

I stay away from auctions, because things are so high that it's hard to resell. You have to ask such crazy prices for them to make any money. I also don't like auctions because things are thrown around in boxes and you really can't look at them. You pay good money for things, and when you get them home you find out they're chipped or cracked, and so you're taking an awful chance at an auction and you can't return them.

I used to do garage sales, too, but they take a lot of time. And there you're gambling because you may run into something and you may not, so you're spending a lot of valuable time just running around, and you better bet that somebody else has gotten there first.

I just sit and wait for someone to call, and they do call because I do a lot of antique shows, and people get to meet me that way and they say, "Well, do you buy?" and I say, "Yes, I buy," and then I get all sorts of calls.

Antique dealers are always told, "This belonged to my great-great-grandmother." People want to get the most they can for something, and I don't care how much you know, you're not an expert on everything, and if you take people's word, when you get the item home, and really take the time to look, you'll often find that it's really not what it was represented to be. Sometimes you can take it back and say you found it was not what you thought it was, but most people will say, "You bought it. It's yours," and that's it. That happens a lot. I feel I've learned a lesson from that—to be more careful. I've got to look at things closely.

I get a lot of private calls from homes, which is where I like to buy because I can look things over and take my time. I get to know people and I make friends that way. When I go somewhere, I say I'll be back in an hour, and my hours turn into three and four and five hours because I sit and talk, and they start to bring things out, and the more they talk, the more they like you and the more they bring out. And they start telling all these fantastic stories. It turns into a great relationship.

I sell mostly to dealers. One who comes up from North Carolina has $20,000 to $30,000 in his pocket. He just goes out and buys and buys. And that's what I'd like to be able to do, buy anything I see, really good-quality stuff. He leaves North Carolina with a big empty truck and stops all along the way. Usually when he gets here he's almost broke, but if I have something he wants, he'll buy. There's all kinds of antiques—very, very inexpensive and very, very expensive. I take him places where he can pick up good stuff that I couldn't afford to buy. For that I get a commission called a finder's fee. I do a lot of that.

If I had to do this for a living right here in this little town, I'd be eating bread and water. I have to get out of this area to sell my antiques, which is why I sell to dealers from Alabama, North Carolina, Michigan, and Canada.

I also do a lot of antique shows. I pack up my best things and take them to a show. People come from all over. The shows cost anywhere from $10 to $100 just for the booth area in which I set up.

If I make $500 to $600 a show, I'm satisfied. I take a variety of things because there are a variety of people looking and collecting different things. I take expensive things and I take things that maybe kids could buy, inexpensive collectibles. I'm there for a few hours, and I make my money fast.

Some days I can sit here, and maybe for two or three days no one shows up, and then one day somebody's going to spend maybe $700 or $800 in less than an hour. I was packing up my wares and going every weekend to a show. It was really tiresome but I loved it.

When I started doing the antique shows, all these people were coming up with these cameras and saying, "Can we take a picture of your booth?" They didn't want a picture of the booth. They wanted a picture of *me* sitting there with all those antiques because there are so few black antique dealers.

I'll put an ad in the paper and when somebody will call me on the phone and say, "Mrs. Bass?" they can't tell that I'm black. I'll ring the doorbell and they'll look surprised—a little bit leery, maybe—but once I'm inside, it's O.K., and they don't want to let me go after that. It's funny to see the surprised looks on their faces when I first arrive. They invite me back. One time I went to help a lady organize a house sale, and I was introduced to her sister-in-law. She looked at me and said, "Oh, I expected a much taller woman," but that's not what she was thinking. She was thinking she didn't expect a black woman. I get those surprised kinds of reactions which are not bad reactions, just surprised.

I love the antiques, and I love the people, and I love the whole idea of doing something for myself that I like. My husband used to call it junk, and now when he sees me making a few dollars, it's not junk any more.

Sister Mary Blosl, O.S.C.*

PRALINE CANDY MAKER,
New Orleans, Louisiana.

A home business can be influenced by certain factors that would not influence a business operated away from home. The presence of other people in the home — sometimes family members, sometimes not — may impose special business hours or space limitations. Even though Sister Mary operates her praline business from a monastery, her business is not inhibited by the Mother Superior or by anyone else living in the monastery.

Our monastery is autonomous in that the sisters here elect someone from among us to be the Mother Superior. She is more a person with us, in the midst of us, instead of somebody on high. Authority used to tell you what to do, but now it consists more of example and living *with* rather than *regulating* from without.

There are 15 sisters here — 94 is our oldest, 30 is our youngest. We live primarily on alms, on the generosity of people; however, we've always been advised to do whatever work we can to supplement what comes in. The handiwork of the sisters takes care of maybe one-eighth to one-tenth of our needs.

*Order of St. Clare (Franciscans).

Years ago I read in a magazine about the poor people of Biafra not having sufficient water in their villages because their water supply was so contaminated that they couldn't use it. I thought, "You know, here I am. I'm a poor woman, but those people don't even have water!" So I started producing praline candy, which is very popular here in the city, and I sent the revenue to the Catholic Charities to be sent to Biafra to alleviate the suffering of those poor people.

I'd put a little sign at the entrance to our monastery. When people came to ask for prayers, when they wanted consolation, or when they wanted a nun to talk to, they'd see the sign in the doorway, Sister Mary's Pralines, and it gave the price.

After about five years, I stopped using the money for the missions and contributed it to the fund of the monastery. The missions' need probably still exists, but after about five years or so, I felt I had done my bit.

Over the years, it has become more of a business than I actually wanted it to. Last year, for example, I made about six batches a day in order to have plenty for our sale right before Christmas, till I thought I'd see them in my sleep. I used to take Christmas orders and send pralines all over the country and the Virgin Islands, to England and to other places. One doctor used to send his whole mailing list here. I'd send pralines to Margaret Mead, the famous anthropologist, because of this doctor. His mailing list had 25 people on it, and he requested about two dozen pralines for each. Well, that gets to be some pralines to package up! Besides those orders, I'd be making pralines to have at the monastery front door. Over the years, I have, of choice, cut back. That's the grand thing about working from home. You can do what you want, when you want, and how you want.

This year I said, "All right. I'll work very hard prior to Christmas, and then I'm not going to make any more until the beginning of the new year. At that time I'll start again to take orders." Now next year, I don't know what I'll be prompted to do.

Since I'm a contemplative nun, my time is divided primarily into periods of prayer and study and religious worship. However, because we are whole beings, it's only natural that I have to *do* something, so a portion of the day is set aside for work. Actually, I have other work to do, too. I'm the bookkeeper for the monastery, and we take turns cooking and maintaining the monastery. I prefer the praline business to be a very small portion of my work time. It's not what I'm here for. I guess creativity is also very much a part of our way of life. We have time to stop and think and look and pray and appreciate. That's what our whole life is about. So creativity is very high on our schedule.

We have a sister who prints and two sisters who sketch and do oil paintings and watercolors. We also have sisters who do beautiful needlework and crochet. I would say that six or seven of us out of the 15 do some creative work.

I work at ceramics sometimes.* I like to do sculpture and original work primarily, but that doesn't bring in as much revenue as the ceramics. Two or three months right before our end-of-the-year sale, I concentrate heavily on doing a lot of ceramic work. That money finances the original work that I want to do throughout the year.

A lot of people down in the French Quarter have asked us, "Please give us some of your things and we'll put them on display down here and sell them," but it's a matter of transporting, of giving them a cut, and they actually ask a big cut. That was why we just set aside one room, right as you come into the entrance here. We have the things on display, and it doesn't matter if they're there two months, three months, six months. We also get the whole profit and, of course, since we're a nonprofit organization, we don't have to worry about taxes. Each of us wants to keep our production small and the best we can produce.

*The dishes in the photograph were made by Sister Mary.

Jane Faul

TYPESETTER AND PRINTER,
Barrington, Illinois.

Local zoning ordinances provide for, regulate, or prohibit home businesses, but we found that some zoning administrators charged with enforcement responsibility were sympathetic and tolerant of victimless violations.

The first time the building inspectors came here was when we were building a running shed on our barn, and then it became just a regular inspection. Another time they came during a Bar Association mailing. We had two tons of materials in the living room, about 12 teenagers collating it, and a big truck outside waiting to take the job into Chicago. Arriving in the middle of this, they asked, "Are you running a business here?" What could I say? They asked if they could make a phone call, and they went into the kitchen. There were two ducks in a box in there because it was a little early in the year and we couldn't put them out yet so the inspectors kept laughing and saying, "Did you see? She's got ducks in the kitchen." The collie was sitting right in the middle of the kids, and one of the cats brought in a snake and was fighting it to the finish. After that, the inspectors turned friendly, and since then we've had no trouble.

I started my secretarial service the same month as my divorce, February 1965. My sister, who was already divorced, was staying here with me with her baby. Sue had one, I had four, and three of them were at home in diapers. We were trading baby sitting and we both had part-time jobs because we couldn't afford to work full time. Housekeepers cost so near to what we could make, we wouldn't have been able to pay the mortgage and also eat, so working in the house started as a matter of necessity. There aren't many ways you can escape four children that small.

Jack Collins, then a loan officer with the First Federal Trust and Savings of Barrington, trusted me when I didn't have a job, had four children, had been ill, and I'd said to him, "I'm going to start a business." All the mortgage institutions I had approached earlier just patted me on the head and said, "That's nice. Come back when you've got it going." Jack stood up for me at a First Federal board meeting and somehow or other got me the mortgage. He can now have any typesetting he wants discounted. His going to bat for me is what permitted me to stay in the house. Of course staying here meant I had to come up with the monthly mortgage payments.

I bought this old Remington typewriter for $65 which I borrowed from my uncle, and I worked for a lawyer and a few other people in the afternoons. Sue waitressed at night.

Those were rough years. I was going to court a lot because my ex-husband kept instituting harassment suits. We went up in front of every judge in Cook County over a four-year period. Finally Judge Hunter said, "If you're going to make a career out of harassing this lady, I'm going to hold jurisdiction, and every time you come up, you're going to come up in front of me and I'm going to hold the money open." Judge Hunter finally raised the child support money, and then the harassment stopped.

I was getting $400 a month in child support and I was making about $140. Minimum subsistence level in 1965 was $634 a month. Sue decided this business was never going to go, so she got out. She made such good money waitressing that my $140 a month didn't look like much to her. She made that in a couple of days. She was right, at the moment, but over the long haul I'm glad that I stuck with it rather than going back to work for someone else.

The secretarial and answering services began the business in the house. Then I moved into press work. I'd type a report all week that paid $120, and I'd run it over to a printer who would run off $460 worth of printing in one afternoon. I decided that I was at the wrong end of this, and so I bought a press.

The first press was a little Model 85 and it cost $1,065. I had $365, so I asked my bank for a $700 loan. The bank where I had banked since I was 15 said, "Let's see now, you're divorced." It was ridiculous that they would begin with my being recently divorced, and it was very discouraging, but they finally did concede to give me the $700. As soon as it was paid off, however, I realized that I had better try a larger press.

As soon as I started running the press, people began asking me to design forms to be typeset, but I didn't know anything about typesetting. It was Bud, a great little guy from IBM, who put me onto this sport. He came in one day when I was typing and said, "If you have that kind of speed, why are you wasting it on a typewriter?" Bud brought in the stand alone composer on a trial basis. It typed such a clear image that I could see it's value at once. I thought, "O.K., I'll take a chance on this." It was a $4,000 machine, and I thought I'd never make enough money to support it. Seven years later, I was working for a $40,000 machine.

I was used to charging by the hour for typing, but I didn't know how to charge for typesetting so I had to figure out what it cost to operate the machine, which included the supplies, the machine's cost, and a person's time to operate it. I decided that the most fair way to bill would be by line count, which I later found was an innovation in the field. The printers thought that was really clever. They got lots lower bills from me than they did from people who would estimate on the total job or by the page, so the printers became very loyal to me.

The customers came by word of mouth. My advertising didn't work at all. I put ads in the paper and nothing happened, so I mailed out little postcards from time to time. That was better. Nothing happened immediately, but people had a tendency to stick them under their desk glass and say, "Well, sometime when we're behind, we might need her." As much as two or three years later, I'd have someone responding to our original postcard.

Senator Graham was very helpful. I had worked for a long time as a volunteer on his campaign. About the second year that I was in business and had expanded and hired women to help me, Senator

Graham brought his secretarial work in here. Then he went around telling people that we were such super girls. Whatever people asked us to do, we did. They could drop work off and forget about it. We could carry it to any step they wanted. If they had their own printer already, that was fine. We could do the key line and paste up and give them galleys. If they didn't, we could do the printing, too.

One of my customers went to California, so we house watched for him and let his dogs out every day, took care of all his mail, secretarial work, phone answering, and post office box. We even placed orders for him. In effect, we ran a branch office for him.

We had another customer who lived nearby and whose dog always ran away. We had his answering service, so when people would call his phone to complain about the dog and I knew he was away, we'd just go find the dog. The children would help with those kinds of tasks.

As the business grew and the children got older, I realized I couldn't do everything, so I brought the family together and said, "We are either going to have to get a housekeeper and move into a condominium and sell our horses or we're all going to have to heave to." So after multiple family votes, we ended up dividing the jobs. The only really basic rule is that whoever cooks doesn't have to do any dishes. They're all good cooks. Liz, in fact, caters parties. She has done our grocery shopping since she was about 10. We would buy a two-week supply and they never would believe at the checkout counter that this child was authorized to buy $140 worth of groceries. We'd make a list of what was essential, and she'd decide on all the rest. She did hit a little heavy on bakery goods for the first few months, but then she realized that that wasn't really the way.

I cook one or two nights a week, and I do dishes when it's my turn, and if my work schedule permits. I supply the money that pays the bills, and they have to contribute labor. We've had votes on this many times when I've had to remind them. "You're not doing your chores!" So far, they've always voted to stay here and do more work.

By the time I decided to go into partnership with David and form a corporation that operated from its own building in town, my business had been built up to where my contribution to the corporation was substantial. I contributed all of the business here at home, other than the typesetting and the two women who worked with me on it. The press went in, and all of the related secretarial supplies and materials. Pamela, one of the secretaries, shifted over to the corporation, as did the answering service and all of the accounts. Even with these contributions, for the first three years, the typesetting supported not only me but also the business. After two and a half years, we achieved our first breakeven year. The business did $170,000 volume last year, and this year we're hoping that it will be $225,000.

When we started the office up in town, it was interesting. I would work here until about 4:00, and then I'd work there until 2:00 or 3:00 in the morning, then come back and start the round over here. David promised to help with the press runs, and I'm sure he probably got in an hour or two a week. When we bought the larger press, I decided that it was time to stop breaking my back, and we got Jerry to run it and then a kid to help him.

David sells, and he pushes me into things that I wouldn't think of doing. I do the day-to-day management and all of the books. I have a tendency not to see over the piles of work in front of me. I'm also the production worker, and he's the one who has more ambition and more interest in getting into new fields. I probably would have quietly sat here typesetting and letting the press sit here unused if it weren't for his saying that it's stupid to have a press and not be running it.

David and I fight frequently. About every three months we break up the partnership, but it has survived five years now, so I suppose it'll survive a while longer. I don't think I'd go into partnership again.

At this point, the corporation continues to provide full services, although the printing is the part that is the most profitable. We maintain the secretarial and the answering services, which are marginally profitable, because when a new business starts up in town, the first thing needed is a part-time secretarial or answering service. Then they say, "By the way, can you run us a letterhead?" and little by little they are old-time customers. As long as we can do all parts of it for them, they're happy, because they don't have to run around finding a whole bunch of little things. It's a supermarket approach to providing everything a small business needs.

In 1979, Jane sold her corporation interests to her partner, David. She continues to operate her typesetting business from her home but plans to retire in two years to the 107-acre farm in Kentucky she bought with money she earned through her business.

I've already got 31 cows down there, and I plan to raise heavy horses as well.

Dorothy M. Swain

FREE-LANCE GRAPHIC ARTIST,
Portland, Oregon.

Women who had children at home frequently expressed frustration over household distractions that caused work stoppages, but they controlled interruptions largely through the organization of time.

It became obvious, after a few years of working, that I needed to set specific goals in order to feel as though I were accomplishing something. Otherwise it was all one grand struggle. Planning my time became extremely important. One of the first things I did was use a spiral notebook to keep track of how much time it took to do the various kinds of work I did during a day, whether housekeeping, business functions, taking care of the children, or doing things for my husband. I kept track of the whole blessed thing minute by minute.

After three or four months, I went back and made summaries in order to understand how I was using my time. I was *not* using it well. I didn't have a good logical plan. From all the research came the first real progress as far as producing work was concerned. I learned how to schedule my day so I was able to accomplish everything that absolutely had to be done—and how to cut out all the things that weren't necessary. For instance, I would do as much housework as

possible between the time I got up in the morning and 9:00 A.M.,
when the children left for school and my husband went to work. At
9:00, I would walk into my studio, shut the door, and stay in there
until the children came home from school about 3:30.

The research also helped me teach my children to operate on a
schedule. They became very independent, more so than if there had
not been a schedule. I think we accomplished a great deal.

I'm an independent free-lance artist. My business is in graphic arts,
that is, artworks that are intended to be duplicated in quantity. It involves illustration primarily. When I was 35 years old, an orthodon-
tist informed us that my ten-year-old son needed $1,500 worth of
work on his teeth over a two-year period. It was far more than we
could ever hope to save and pay for in that length of time. I immediately took a job at a print shop in a publishing house and learned
how the entire process worked from start to finish, which included
learning thirteen different machine operations. I also learned what
kind of artwork came into the shop and what had to be done in order
to make it work on the presses. The printer and the owner of the
shop said that *most* artists didn't know anything about the processes
involved.

After two and a half years of making 57¢ an hour, I realized that I
was not going to be paid any more money, nor was I being paid any
more for overtime, no matter how inconvenient it was for me. I went
to work in a display department of a fashion house. There I received
$1.27 an hour for carrying 75-pound dummies up and down two
flights of marble stairs to decorate fourteen large windows every two
weeks. The young man who was my immediate superior was an absolute genius at decorating and display. I received the equivalent of a
college education working with him. However, after I worked there
over two years, the company decided I had not earned my vacation,
after doing all of his work and mine, during a period when he was off
for his five-week summer military encampment. I decided I needed a
vacation more than they needed my help. I went home and cried
alone because I was so angry.

I pulled myself together and decided to go into business on my
own. No more of this nonsense of working for other people at low
pay and in terrible conditions. I might just as well use all the talent I
had to start my own business. It was a terrible shock to my husband

to have my share of our income subtracted so suddenly, but he realized I was in earnest. I honestly don't think he thought I would be any kind of success at what I wanted to do. He laid down a set of very strict but, I feel, wise rules.

First of all, I was to get no financial help from his income whatsoever. That money was dedicated to keeping the family together and providing for the children. If I wanted to buy equipment and materials and do all the things that are required in a business, I had to finance it myself out of what I could earn myself. Second, I was not to hire anyone. He didn't want to have the obligation of paying someone else's salary if I was not going to be a success in the beginning. Third, I was not to pay a commission to anyone, particularly to an agent, representative, or dealer. If I was going to sell my work, I had to learn to sell it myself and keep all of the earnings for myself. Fourth, he insisted that I open a separate bank account so there would be no confusion between the family income and my business income. Last, he wanted to make sure there was a good record for tax reporting at the end of the year. After this discussion, he had no more to say about it. He didn't want to know what I was doing or how I was doing, except when we did the bank statement once a month.

I soon found there was a great deal I didn't know about the business world. Operating a business on one's own is quite different from working for other people. In the beginning, I was very poor at reading, and worse at arithmetic, but I learned because I had a really solid reason to learn—to make my business grow.

I think one of the most difficult parts of starting a business, in those days, was that there was so little written material available for women. Even the material for men was not oriented toward artwork of the kind I did. I knew no other women or men who did it. The one thing I needed to hear most was that it was possible to do what I had set out to do, but no one said, "It's entirely possible. . . . Others have done it." I was a pioneer in everything I did. Once I had launched my business, however, everyone in my family pitched in and gave as much encouragement as they could. They all thought it was delightful that I was going to use my art talent, but they never told me that they thought I would be a success.

Since I don't drive, I walked in a ten-block circle around my house to meet people in small businesses. I figured it would be far easier for them to come to me and find parking close to where I lived, rather than for me to have to go to the business district to pick up and deliver the work. Most of these people were exceptionally friendly. They were surprised to have someone in their own area available to do the graphic artwork they needed.

I had a total of $5 cash and a stock of art materials I had accumulated over the years, which came as gifts from people in the family, particularly my father. It was a matter of spending that $5 very carefully, penny by penny, until I earned my first income from sales, then learning to use *that* money to finance the next part of my business until I made more income. It was very hard for me to figure out whether to spend $1.20 on one piece of cardboard, or if I could get along with a 90¢ piece. Art materials do not cost very much money in comparison to raw materials in some other businesses, but if you have so little money to start with, it seems like 25¢ is a monumental amount to spend for one pencil that you grind up in a sharpener!

There were times when I needed to buy materials in order to complete a job, but I didn't have enough cash on hand to buy them outright. I would have to ask a store owner to trust me for the period of time it would take me to complete the job, get paid, and reimburse him. Some of the businesses refused to do that. It seemed like such a comparatively small amount of money to them. They couldn't believe that anyone would need to borrow on credit in that way. After being turned down a few times, I simply made it plain to my clients that, if their job required me to buy more material than I had on hand, they would first have to give me a retainer to cover the cost of that material; otherwise there was no way I could complete their work.

I knew nothing about contracts and very little about collections. All of these things had to be learned, one mistake at a time. One practice common in all areas of business, not just in artwork, but in most retail, wholesale, and industrial businesses, is that major suppliers or clients don't pay their bills promptly. In fact, the common practice is to hold off paying as long as possible. I pay every single account when it is due, and no longer than ten days beyond the account date. I never let a balance go 30 days in arrears, because I feel it's an unethical practice.

At first I thought there was something wrong with my work if clients were not paying promptly. Eventually I came to understand that my work was perfectly satisfactory and it was rather that the owners of a business will not pay bills until absolutely necessary. The longer they can stall off paying someone, the more money they have with which to operate. If it's in a savings account, they're earning interest. If it's used in other ways for business, it's earning them direct income.

More than half of my clients wait from 30 to 120 days to make payments due me. I have to carry those accounts for that period of time, operating on my savings, rather than on current income. If I have to threaten to collect from someone, who can well afford to pay my small fee, I am running the risk of losing the client. That means I have to go out and find someone else to take their place in my client rolls. In the last ten years, only four clients have skipped on their payments and left town.

I've also found it difficult to deal with reprint thefts. Several times my artwork has been cut out of local publications and reprinted in other publications without any payment to me or to the buyer who owned the original copyright. It's nothing but thievery. Another problem I face as a free-lance artist is the general lack of understanding by the public about what artists do, how long it takes to accomplish work, and what the real costs are of producing graphic art.

When dealing with the small businesses in my immediate area in the suburbs, I was limited to black-and-white work, so I decided to operate my business in an independent studio in the city center. I wanted more chance to work in color. I needed an opportunity to experiment in that area, and I believed I could do it if I had a larger studio space and more clients.

Moving to the center of the city again had a staggering effect on our income. I lost half of the clients that I'd had in my suburban area. The same reason was given by each client for not using my business any longer. It took too long to drive into the city center and to find a parking space.

When I moved out of my home and downtown I found the overhead was more than double what I had allowed myself for overhead at home. I had to reorient my entire thinking and develop different kinds of goals. I had to devise a new advertising system and contact clients I had never met before. I was fortunate to have it come out so well. There was a time, shortly after I had moved downtown, when I had only $23 in my account after paying my bills. I wasn't sure I'd make it through the month, but I did make it and I increased my client list. I also increased my prices.

Today, I have as many as 150 clients per year. Other artists I've met in the last few years, who operate this kind of business, have as few as two or three clients—many have ten or 12—but I know of only a few others who operate with as many different clients as I do. Since most of my clients are small-business people, I must have more clients in order to make an adequate income for myself.

I wanted to try architectural rendering. Since I started with little knowledge of basic mathematics, it was an odd choice for me to have made, but I enjoy a challenge and I love geometry. I made contacts with the American Institute of Architects where the women in charge of the office were more than helpful in directing business to me, and now architectural renderings comprise about 40% of my income. I find it most satisfying work.

A couple of years ago my husband had a heart attack, and he is now permanently retired on a disability pension. That changed our lifestyles completely. Again I reoriented my goals. I've cut my hours of studio work in order to spend more time with him. If I had to leave it all today to spend the last few days with him, I *would*, because I find I cherish him more than *ever* after 35 years of marriage. He doesn't want me to stop doing what I do, although he's allowed me to slow down somewhat. Although he never asked me to quit in earlier years, he was tempted.

We nearly went crazy the first few months he was unemployed, because he had previously worked such a heavy schedule—12 to 16 hours a day. Suddenly he had nothing to do and I was afraid it would kill him. Gradually we have reversed roles. He now takes care of the house, and he is finding joy in something *new*. He is learning about my business.

Two years later, Dorothy wrote:

Got two assignments to do courtroom sketching for a local television station: (1) union labor vs. U.S. government, and (2) wife vs. husband rape case of national interest (Rideout case). Hard work, but good pay, and very interesting. Landed my first government contract to illustrate for the Forest Service. It's a several months' job, and they paid off the other day. First time I ever connected with a bid.

For information contact: Dorothy M. Swain, Commercial Illustration Studio Gallery, Suite 300, Oekum Building, 519 S.W. Third Street, Portland, Oregon 97204.

Dr. Susan Cropper

VETERINARIAN HOUSE CALL SERVICE
FOR DOGS AND CATS,
Wyckoff, New Jersey.

Three-fifths of the women we interviewed had to coordinate family responsibilites with the operation of their businesses. They often described how each conflict had to be resolved individually.

I have one child who is eight. When I was doing the farm calls, she was eight months old and she went with me in the cab of my truck. I had an aide who worked with me and we both fed her and took care of her as we practiced. She goes with me now every once in a while. When she was very small, I was working in a hospital until 8:00 or 9:00 P.M. Consequently, she slept till noon every day and then stayed up till midnight or 1:00 A.M. with us so that we could enjoy her. It was a normal schedule just moved up a little bit.

I can't be a functional parent or a functional doctor unless I first consider what I want. When I don't do that, I don't do anything as well. I think everybody's like that.

I like the way my life is. I'm a veterinarian with some degree of confidence, and I practice with a whole lot of enjoyment. People tell me how marvelous it is that I make house calls. It isn't marvelous. I simply do a service that used to be available before we became so mechanized. Because the service is generally not available, people talk about it.

It's a super thing for women to do. People are receptive to a woman veterinarian who makes house calls because there's not the threat of a man coming into the home when a woman is alone. That problem shouldn't exist, but it does. A man would not find himself as readily accepted.

I am continually delighted with the people whom I meet and can help. There's the older woman who is ill and can't go out of the house except maybe once a month to go to the doctor. Her husband has a heart condition and can't drive. They can't ask somebody to take their cats in and then wait at the office until the cats are ready to come home. It's especially rewarding for me to help such people.

It's also sometimes beneficial for me to see an animal's environment so I can take that into account in my diagnosis and treatment. For instance, the dog I'll be seeing this afternoon has a problem with his back. Many times such a problem is aggravated by having to go downstairs. Twice I've sat in people's homes and heard them say, "There aren't any stairs that my dog has to go on." Yet I'm sitting in the family room, and from the family room to the rest of the house there are three steps going up. It's not much, but it can be a lot to the dog, and the people never saw it. It isn't something that I would have been able to know about if I hadn't been in their home.

Then, too, people tend to feel that if there are half-a-dozen people waiting in an office, they should hurry through their questions. I went to a pediatrician who always made me feel that I was taking up more of his time than he possibly had to give me. Since I knew he was busy, I didn't ask him some of the questions that I wanted to ask about my daughter. Sometimes there is more conversation than is necessary, but it's better to have more than not enough.

In addition, when I was practicing from an office, probably every fifth person would say to me, "I have a stupid question to ask you." Now that happens only once in a while because people are relaxed enough to be able to ask what they want to ask. If you don't know the answer, it's not a stupid question.

I expected at the beginning that there would be a lot of problems with things that happen in offices, such as frightened animals who relieve themselves or express their anal sacs or try to chew my face off—but there haven't been many. The animals recognize who I am right away and realize that I'm helping them.

Like many young girls, I wanted to be a veterinarian. I was encouraged by my parents even though at that time it was almost impossible for a woman to get admitted to veterinary school. Through a combination of fortuitous occurrences, and a lot of prayer, a lot of wishing, and a lot of studying in between, I was accepted the first time I applied—but if I hadn't been accepted, I'd have applied again until I eventually wore them down.

I had always intended to go into a small-animal practice. I did a year of practice close to the town where I had grown up, and then I went back and taught at the veterinary school where I graduated. After that, I wound up in a small town in Indiana working for a practitioner in a capacity that just wasn't working out, and I felt that it was necessary to have my own practice.

I had a hospital and I did dogs and cats, which would have been my primary interest, except that my husband was still in school and I couldn't support us that way, so I became a large-animal practitioner making rural farm calls. I did horses and chickens and pigs and goats and whatever else there was. At that point I acquired a mobile veterinary clinic in which I had hot and cold running water, a refrigerator, a freezer, places where the drugs were heated and cooled, and a hose so I could wash the unit down. It was a magnificent unit. The bank, my husband, and I financed it. However, instead of borrowing enough money to open the practice properly, I borrowed as little as I could, and so I was always a little bit behind.

Because I was new in business, and wanted it to succeed so badly, I went far out of my way to be of benefit to clients, but did not insist that they pay me. I found it very hard to discuss money with them. That should be a thing that the schools teach. Money makes it possible for you to stay around and be of service to people. I didn't go into medicine to make money but because I cared about animals, and money was secondary. When clients called me because their animals were ill, I didn't feel that I couldn't go, and they knew that, and many called me who never intended to pay me. I subsidized their animals. I cared more for their animals than they did. When my husband got a job here, I left Indiana with close to $10,000 in outstanding balances that I was never going to get.

It's profitable for me to make house calls. I could make more money in a regular practice, but the only way that I'd want to continue being a veterinarian is if I was happy with the amount of money that I brought in as well as with the rewards of doing the practice. I charge the same fees basically as most practitioners, but I charge an additional fee for the house call which I tell my clients about before I see them. I'm limited in the fact that I can make only five to six stops in a day's time. I work on a cash or check basis and I do no billing. I will never be in a medical practice again where I do billing. It's not necessary. If you can pay the plumber, you can pay the doctor. Many times I will allow people to give me postdated checks, and I'll hold them until they can meet the payment. I get a lot of referrals from other practitioners in the area. Some of what I get is people who call who have a big nasty dog that they're afraid to take in the car. When I was in practice in a hospital, I would have been thrilled to death to have somebody I could refer my clients to—"Call her. She'll go see your dog"—and I get some of those. I have scars from some of them but most of those that are aggressive in the office are not as aggressive at home, fortunately.

I have to have a certain degree of sureness in order to get the owner of the animal to help me. One girl said, "We can't put a muzzle on this dog," and I said, "Sure we can." I could see her think, "Oh, all right," and then she did it. That dog didn't want me to be even close to it. All she had to do was to get it to where it was restrained enough that it wasn't going to take a piece out of me, and at that point I could take it over from her.

I have two stresses: the stress of the animal patient that doesn't get better as it's supposed to and the stress of the owner's fear that the animal isn't going to get better. There ought to be a rule guaranteeing that an animal will respond to medicine by getting better.

Fear is something that any medical practitioner deals with. "It's 14. I've lived with it all of its life. Is it going to die?" I have lapses when I'm not confident, and that's understandable, because I don't have all the answers, but I know what I can accomplish.

If I know an animal's going to die, I tell them just that. People who have older animals, who know that it's time to put them to sleep, want to have it done at home. And I understand that. I put a dog of mine to sleep a little over a year ago—a big St. Bernard with bone cancer. We had done what there was to do. It was time. It's time with them just as sometimes it's time with us. I use an overdose of the same anesthetic I inject for surgery. I can do it myself, which amazes me even in saying it, because it was not possible to do it that way in the hospital. People bring in an animal and it's agitated and you have to have another pair of hands to help hold it.

Sometimes I need to sedate the animals, and sometimes I need to ask the people to help, but I don't want them to remember that part. I want them to remember whatever life the animal has had. So I go somewhere where I can be alone with the animal, and we discuss it, the animal and I, and most of the time the animal is ready. I think there's too much order in all the things that I know about for this to be the only shot at life than any of us get. I think we go around until we get it right, and think the animals do, too. That's clearer to me since I started doing the house calls, because they're home and some of them are ready to die. When they're ready to die, they don't struggle. You sometimes have to take the choice away from those that aren't ready, so the animal won't suffer. Do the people cry and feel bad? Yes, they cry and feel bad. These are people who care about their animals.

It has always been suggested that doctors not get too involved with their patients. I don't know how to practice medicine without getting involved with patients. The more rapport I can have with the people whom I deal with, the more they'll tell me and the better diagnosis I can make. The better diagnosis I can make, the better treatment I can give and the more quickly the patient will get better—and that's what it's all about.

Dr. Jeanne Leslie

PEDODONTIST,
Tenafly, New Jersey.

Women with children who could afford full-time help found that it permitted them to pursue their businesses relatively unencumbered, but it didn't mean that their life was problem-free or that full-time help was the best solution.

Originally we had full-time help, which was good when the children were little so that I was freer. Meals were on time, and help was much easier to find at that time. As the children grew older, there wasn't as much need, and we objected to the invasion of our privacy. When matters start to build up, somehow you get a little more organized and things seem to work out very well.

My priorities have changed. It used to be children first, and slowly, over the years, I'm beginning to learn that mother is number one, and that's new, very new. Somehow now that I'm a lot happier, I find my children are a lot happier. You sort of set up a climate of happiness and they fall into it. Women tend to get trapped and certainly people of my generation married forever and accepted whatever came along. It took a lot of get-up-and-go after 22 years for me to say. "No, this is not what I want. There must be a better way." But I have no regrets—and you go from day one.

I came from a medical background. My father is a physician, my brother, everybody down the line. It was "You're bright, you have to do something. You have to use your mind." It never was a question of *if* you're going to college, but where you're going and what are you going to be? I thought I wanted to be a pediatrician like my father. I wanted to work with children, so I made the alternate list at New York University Medical School. The boys were coming back from military service right after the war, and it was very difficult to get into medical school. I had several uncles who were dentists and they said, "Why don't you try dental school?" I was accepted in ten days, so I decided, "O.K. I'll be a dentist."

Dentistry is a fantastic field for a woman. You make your own hours. There are emergencies, but they don't happen frequently, and nobody dies, which is very good. I also found that dentistry works in very well with a family. If you want to take off on Monday, take off on Monday; just don't schedule appointments. Whenever my children were on vacation, I didn't open the office, so I was off all summer, Christmas vacations, Easter vacations, and whenever the children were off.

I also found that, for my particular personality, dentistry worked out better than pediatrics as far as children go. The thing I do best is what we call patient training, and it's the thing I enjoy most. We use no tranquilizers or anesthesia. The new pedodontists don't practice the way I do. I am a dying breed. They use more medication and more anesthesia, which are certainly easier on the dentist. I don't believe in it. In this drug-ridden society, I'm loath to put a child on drugs or gas just to calm him down. A lot of children don't like it. I learned a long time ago that if you tell them what's going on they can handle it. When a child screams and cries, that doesn't bother me at all. I get more upset with mothers who interfere. If I can reach the mothers, then it's fine. I do the talking and they do the listening. They are allowed in the room because I feel that that gives support. With the mother present, it's clear that it has to be done, it's going to be done. This is a statement I use constantly: "It has to be done, it's going to be done, and Dr. Leslie's going to do it. You get the choice of what color toothpaste you want or whether your mother can stay in the room with you."

My father had two ways of making an appointment: everybody came at either 1:00 or 2:00 o'clock. They would bring their lunch and their diapers, the office was crowded, and they would sit there until 5:00 o'clock. When I opened my office, I decided that was not the way to run an office. I wanted it run by appointment, so if anything, we underbook. I find that a child sitting there and waiting becomes more and more tense. The dog has been a godsend. The children play with Munchkin, my little black dachshund that wanders in and out, and one child once said to me, "Is this your kitchen?" We talk back and forth from one room to another, and the wall is covered with pictures the children have drawn. Some of them are interesting: "I love you, but I don't like what you do!" "I like you, but I don't like the drill." My favorite one says, "Happy birthday to a very nice friend and a good dentist. You may be old, but you're not grouchy."

I enjoy children, and they know it. They cannot be fooled. One of the reasons my practice is successful is because it's in the home and the children patients don't feel they are going to an office building. When I initially thought about opening an office, it was suggested that I go into an office building because the practice would grow more quickly, and I'm sure that that is true. For my purposes, it was not what I wanted. I was not as motivated to work from a large office as I was in providing a service, doing what I wanted, and having it grow the way I wanted. I'm very glad the office is here. The character of my practice would change if I were in an office building. There would be no kitchen to run to and come back with a spoonful for the mother to taste. It would lose some of the casualness that I seem to require.

Dentistry is a physically enervating profession, particularly if you give it your all, and there are times you can get very uptight. I was in general practice at one time for about six months, and I found that I was more tired at the end of the day working with adults that I am working with children.

Children who come into the office size me up, and I size them up. That's the way it goes. If you're O.K., you're going to make it with me. When I'm not feeling quite myself, I'll send a patient home because they get the wave, particularly when you work with a lot of two-year-olds.

Originally I got my patients by word of mouth. Now that I'm in a different position, with a divorce pending, I've been enlarging the practice by letting it be known that I want more patients. I started going to the Bergen County Dental Association, in which I have become fairly active, and I'm on the Executive Council of the New Jersey pedodontists and the Children's Dental Society. Most of my patients come from referrals by other dentists and now from other patients. I've allowed the practice to mushroom, and while frankly a home office is not ideal for a tremendously large practice, I'm not ready to move out because all I need is a little more. I don't want to work that hard. I work hard enough as it is, and I like what I do. I'm not money motivated. It's taken me a long time to learn that accepting money or asking for money is part of a business. I was brought up in a professional family, and the money was nice, but the philosophy was "I'd rather wait for the money." I find that most people are honest, but we do get stuck because of a laissez faire attitude.

When I first opened, a young man in the area said, "Why don't you come in with me and I guarantee you'll make $100,000. I'm going to be the biggest dentist in the area." And I said to him, "We differ right there because I just want to be the best."

Judy S. Krassner

SUMMER CAMP AND TRIP COUNSELOR FOR
CHILDREN AND TEENAGERS,
Northbrook, Illinois.

The third year was the key year for most of the women. At that point, the overwhelming majority of those we interviewed were either rethinking their business situation or looking toward significant expansion. Judy Krassner found herself questioning how the business was fitting into her life as a whole.

I guess I suddenly realized that I wasn't soaring. Now I'm going into the third season. My wings are clipped, and I've come down to earth a little bit. Even though I've really started making money, I feel a let down, and I wonder why I feel this way. Maybe it's just a normal reaction. For a while, I felt, "What do I need this for?" Then I came to the conclusion, Yes, I want to do this. Now I'm reassessing: What do I qualify as success—quality? quantity? or a combination of both? I'm obviously not willing to sacrifice quality, but do I have the energy to do the necessary ongoing research and checking up and making sure that the kids really did have a good time and that the directors of the trip or camp really did do what they promised to do?

I'm an independent representative for Student Camp and Trip Advisors of Boston. I sit down and chat with a family about the best possible summer experience for their youngster for this particular summer. Of course, whether or not youngsters are ready to go to camp depends on their background. I know 8-year-olds who are ready, but there are 15-year-olds who've never been away from home who can't handle it. The breaking-away process should be gradual. It can't happen suddenly—boom!—when they're 17 or 18.

My clientele are people who feel that their children's summers are an extension of their education. Since the programs they choose are usually, but not always, expensive, my business must be in a well-to-do area.

Fathers are rarely involved. They sign the check and they don't know what's happening with the youngster. If I call back and get a father, I'd do just as well to hang up and call another time. They don't even know what their wife has decided or what the youngster is talking about or what I'm talking about or who I am.

It was April 1976 when I started advertising. The season starts in September, but there's much leg work to do between September and April: publicity to line up, people to see, new camps, old camps, and follow-up with all the kids. The first year was an outgo investment, yet I was delighted with the results. Over the summer I visited the different situations where I had youngsters placed. It turned out that my only vacation month, really, is August. Weekends in midwinter are very busy because directors come through town. One weekend a couple of weeks ago, five directors were in town at the same time over a four-day weekend. At other times, I'll have reunions at the house for kids and directors.

Most people who run camps and trips are highly ethical and dedicated. They are usually educators, and you have to have a love for kids to put up with the kids and parents and want to make them happy. Once in a while, a director will present his situation in a certain light in order to get the kids to his camp or on his trip and then won't produce what he promises. But it is very difficult to prove.

If several different people tell me about the same kind of an incident, I can be pretty sure it happened. If the director is interested, I'll tell him. If he doesn't care, then there's not much I can do except not recommend him in the future. For instance, the director of a camp where I've sent a few kids in the past years has absolutely incredible skills and an excellent staff, but in the evenings the camp is totally unsupervised. That's not a situation that I choose to represent.

One reason I'm able to pursue the business so successfully is because my husband is very sympathetic. I think that within the structure of a successful marriage, if you don't have a husband who is at least sympathetic with what you want to do, you'll have a hard time doing it. Like for instance, I had an appointment at the airport the other day, the day of an ice storm. My husband piled his brief-case in the car so he could work while I was talking and he drove me there. It's this kind of thing that is really beyond the call of duty that gives me the extra little help that sometimes you need to keep the contacts.

If I tell him that I have appointments in the evening, people are coming in at 7:30, he'll either make an effort to get home early or he won't worry if we don't have dinner. The nitty-gritty domestic aspects have become very unimportant to both of us, and if they weren't that way, then my business is something I would find difficult to do.

Where do I want to take this business? I know that I can take it to the limits of my physical capabilities. How much of my time do I really want to invest in the business at this point? I think there comes a point somewhere along the line where you can work with only a certain number of people and, beyond that, you can't keep it personalized. So what has to go? How much do I turn over to an assistant?

In an hour's time with a youngster, although I really don't know that child, I do have an overall feeling of what kind of kid I'm talking to and how this kid functions in a family situation. Because of the research I've done, knowing the personalities of the directors, knowing their physical setups, what kind of people they hire, and what they do, I can tell where this child will fit in well and be happy.

Yet, how many hundreds of kids can I meet with, service, and know in a year? That's what I'm rethinking. What I'm going to do is what is comfortable.

A year later, Judy told us:

My business has expanded so much, and I have personally expanded with it. I've become so well organized, I can easily handle the increased growth of the business. I have a part-time assistant who helps me, and because of what she does, I am left free to work with people. I now really feel on top of the situation.

For information write Judy Krassner, Student Camp and Trip Advisors, 1845 Mission Hills Lane, Northbrook, Illinois 60062.

Blanche H. Dick

BEAUTICIAN,
Idaho Falls, Idaho.

Most of the women didn't regard themselves as having accomplished anything special, although many of them have produced beautiful work or, with extraordinary perseverance, have succeeded in providing a living for themselves and family through their home business. One such woman is Blanche Dick, who supports herself and raised her family through a small home beauty shop. She had never responded to our initial inquiry, but she remembered our letter asking if she'd be a subject for our study when we knocked on her door one Sunday afternoon.

I really don't think I have much to offer. I've just got a little tiny business.

As was true with many of the other women who worked from home, Blanche conducted her business with a sensitivity toward her clientele that went even beyond the usual attentiveness practiced by small businesses. Besides going to senior-citizen homes and hospitals to do the hair of her long-time clients, Blanche picks up those who still live at home but are unable to get to her place by themselves.

I hate to have them take a taxi. It's so expensive both ways.

They're all my friends. It's just like one big family the way we do it.

When my husband passed away I was left with three little children, so I had to make a living at something. I debated whether to be a practical nurse or a beautician, and I thought I'd have too much night work if I was a nurse. Mrs. Roberry, who went to the same church as I did, talked me into going to beauty school. She knew that I had to make my living and take care of my children at the same time. I was a worrywart all the time and kept saying, "What will I do when I get through school?" "Well now," she said, "you know that you can work here"—and she gave me a job in the salon. That was in 1950.

I worked there for over two years, and then I remarried and came home. After I'd been married four years, I had Dennis, this little boy, and that's when I decided to go back to work. My second husband and I separated. I'd take Dennis with me, and we got along like that until he got old enough so that I could leave him at nursery school. The other children were already old enough. The youngest of them was 15 when Dennis was born. When Dennis was 6 years old, I decided to come home and fix the shop here so I would be home when he came home from school.

I had this little room, but I had to have another one built on. Even though I had the equipment, it cost me about $1,000 to move home. I borrowed the money from my mother. The worst thing was the worry that if I came home, I wouldn't do enough to make a living, but it worked out really well. The city lets me have the business in my home as long as I don't hire any help.

I was so busy I didn't know whether I could handle all my clients, and you know, it's always been that way. I've had a good clientele, and they just stayed with me. One tells a friend, and I do it all by appointment. I don't have any drop-ins.

It's really much more profitable here than in the shop because we had to pay so much rent there. I was with another lady and we each paid half, but at home I don't have the overhead. I have to keep up my home and everything, but it's not like paying the really high rent. I love it here. I'd really hate to have to go back into a shop. I'm not rich, but I make a good living—more than if I went out and worked for wages.

I've done as many as 17 shampoos and waves in a day, but usually I do an average of ten shampoos and maybe one permanent.

I'm not a hairstylist, just a hairdresser, and I don't like to do fancy hair styles, so I don't do very many. I have some people with long hair, but I wouldn't take any new ones.

I book my customers every half hour. The first of the week, there are more permanents. I do tinting, but I don't do bleaching any more. I think women are better off to go in a big shop where they have the machinery. I used to do manicures, but I don't have time to do those any more, so I don't do them, either.

I work Monday through Friday from 8:00 to 6:00 and on Saturdays until about 2:00. I work on Sundays only if there's an emergency, but otherwise no. Some clients come every other week, but most of them come once a week. Many of them say they like to come here because they don't like to go downtown. They also don't like to be in a big shop where there's lots of noise and confusion, and here they don't have to dress up. It's just friendly, and they can relax.

I got a TV put in here because a lot of times women would call up and when I'd suggest a time, they'd say, "Oh, I can't come in because my show is on." So I said, "Well, now I've a TV." They've got some earphones and they can listen even under the dryer, so that works out pretty well.

Most of the neighbor ladies are clients of mine, but I also have customers who come from downtown and all over, even some who live right by other beauty shops. Mostly they come because I've done their hair for a long time. A new shop started nearby on Fourteenth Street, but it hasn't hurt my business because it has a different clientele. I do more older ladies. They weren't so old when we started, but they've grown a lot older. A man who came to fix my house one day asked, "How come yours are so old?" and I said, "Well, we all got old together." I've done a lot of my clients for 25 years. Some have such a limited income that I just can't charge them what I do regularly, and in general, because of my lower overhead, I don't charge as much as the big shops. I'll never get rich because I don't have the heart to charge them. Some of them are in rest homes now. I try to do their hair sometimes, but I'm so busy here with just me, I can't leave often.

All the rest homes have a little beauty shop with dryers, and they have a beauty operator, but my long-time customers want me to come when they move into a rest home. I also still have about three or four now that I pick up and drive home, but so many of them are gone.

I used to pick up and bring back a little lady who was so ill that she had to have a pacemaker and walk with a cane. Now she's over in the rest home, and the other day she called me and said, "This is the first time I've really been able to make a phone call. My hair is looking bad. When can you come and give me another permanent?" The daughter-in-law of another lady who just had a stroke and now is in a wheelchair asked me if I'd do her mother-in-law's hair because they wanted it to be as near like she always had it to make her feel better. I went down there and, honestly, you just can't believe it. I could hardly understand her. They sit in those wheelchairs, and you wonder if they even know what's going on, and yet they're 100% better and so much happier when they get their hair done. They pat your hand to let you know. It's just amazing.

I always have to do it in the evenings when the rest home's beauty shop isn't busy. I try to go just as soon as I get through work here, so it won't be too late, because they go to bed at 8:00. I usually try to get there by 6:30.

And another thing, I go to funeral homes, too—mainly for the ladies whose hair I have done for a long time. I just pin them up the night before, and then go in the morning and comb them out. It's really no problem. I feel bad because it's always somebody I know, but I get the satisfaction of knowing I can make them look as they would want to look. One lady made me promise, "Now when I die, I want you to be sure and do my hair. I don't want somebody else to." So I promised her that if I was still around, I would—and sure enough. . .

When my children were little I used to give them permanents. Blayne was telling somebody one day, "Yeah, my mother used to, and I looked like Elvis Presley." I had it really quite curly until they got older, then they wouldn't let me. By the time they got to be 12 or 14 they didn't care for it. No more permanent waves. I used to have a good time giving them all permanents. I used to think it looked real cute, but they tell me now that they didn't think it was so great.

We asked Blanche what it's like at Christmas time, and she said:

At Christmas time, you just can't believe it! All kinds of cookies, candies, and cakes, and then gifts, like stationery and, oh, I've gotten necklaces. And last year I got a pretty chain necklace, silver on one side, and pens or little whatnots. I offer the cakes and candies in the shop, but it seems like they don't want to eat them much. They say they're for me.

Index

Capitalized entries refer to the occupations profiled in each segment.